THE LIFE OF LULA

PEDRO SANTOS

OPPIAN

The Life of Lula

By Pedro Santos

ISBN 978-951-877-935-6

© Oppian Press
Helsinki, 2023

CONTENTS

A CHILD IS BORN

TEARS OFTEN MARK the beginning or end of a compelling story. In this instance, they serve as a prelude to a human life entering the world. Specifically, in the year 1945, in the northeastern district of Caetés, Brazil. This is the tale of Lula, Brazil's three-time president, which intertwines significantly with the struggles of millions of Brazilians battling poverty and inequality.

Located in the northeastern region of Brazil, the Agreste region of Pernambuco presents numerous challenges for its residents. Relentless heat, drought, and scarce natural resources exacerbate the difficulties faced by its inhabitants. Furthermore, the region has endured centuries of exploitation by colonizers, ranging from the Portuguese and Dutch to the Jesuits and later the cocoa barons. Throughout Brazil's history, the northeast has known no peace.

Within this backdrop, a child is born. Luiz Inácio da Silva, the fifth of seven siblings, enters the world mired in poverty. Life expectancy in the region is a mere 35 years. The nickname "Lula," which would eventually become an official part of his name, would come into prominence years later.

Lula's mother, known as Dona Lindu, shoulders the responsibility of raising her children amidst countless hardships. Lula's father, Aristides Inácio da Silva, abandoned her while she was pregnant with Lula to marry and start a family with her cousin. Despite this, Aristides supports both families for many years. Lula only meets his father when he is already five years old.

In 1952, Dona Lindu, with little to her name, sells her belongings and embarks on a 13-day journey with her seven children, including one-year-old Sebastiana. They sustain themselves during the trip with brown sugar and a sugar bar, commonly used in the region to alleviate hunger. Their destination is Guarujá, a city near Santos in the interior of São Paulo state. Interestingly, Santos is the city where Pelé, the athlete of the century, later migrates to.

Lula's relationship with his father is fraught with difficulties. The delayed introduction at the age of five and the challenges of living in two families mark the beginning of a tumultuous period of family problems in their impoverished environment.

During the subsequent years when both of Aristides' families reside in Guarujá, violence becomes a regular part of Lula's life. Paradoxically, Aristides ensures that his extensive brood never goes hungry, yet he inflicts regular and increasingly brutal beatings upon his children. One such incident involves Lula's older brother and a chain. If not for Lindu's intervention, the outcome could have been fatal.

When Aristides assaults Dona Lindu, who had severed all romantic ties upon discovering his other family, she promptly moves out with her children. They lose their daily provisions but gain safety. What use is a satiated hunger if the flesh bleeds?

Three years later, Lindu migrates once again with her children, this time to the state capital, São Paulo. The city stands as Brazil's most important economic and populous center, earning the title of the country's economic capital and the most populous city in the southern hemisphere. The year is 1955.

Lula, who began his school studies, was compelled to abandon them to accompany his mother and siblings into the urban landscape. In São Paulo, they lived in close quarters, occupying a cramped room at the rear of a bar. One vivid memory for Lula was the shared restroom in the bar, which was frequented by intoxicated patrons and confronted with unsightly sights such as vomiting. However, they found solace in the absence of violence within the home.

INDUSTRIAL LIFE

THE IPIRANGA DISTRICT, where Lula and his family resided, bordered an industrial region that would later be recognized as the "ABC Paulista," a crucial industrial hub with a significant labor force, ultimately shaping the future president's trajectory. Despite hardship and adversity, Mrs. Lindu, with unwavering love and care, continued to tend to her children.

Years later, Lula made an attempt to return to school, facing the academic year with only three pieces of clothing, two of which served as sleepwear. While his performance was commendable in subjects like general knowledge and communication, he struggled in scientific disciplines. The following year, he decided not to pursue further education.

During his adolescence, football entered the picture. While for many nations it is just a sport, in Brazil, it serves as an escape from poverty and a vital socialization mechanism. Football in Brazil is primarily played in open spaces with natural, untended grass or sand, in backyards, vacant lots, and deserted squares, where individuals of all ages come together for matches that have fewer regulations and a more aggressive style, nurturing numerous talented players. From Pelé to Neymar, all have been initiated in the grassroots football culture and honed their skills amidst the financial challenges of an inherently unjust nation.

Lula exhibited great aptitude on the field, but his skills in management and leadership surpassed his prowess with the ball at his feet. He became the "owner" of the ball, organizing matches and resolving disputes. Often, these conflicts were settled in a traditional manner seen in Brazilian street football, involving minor acts of violence such as punches and kicks. Although not the eldest or the strongest among the teams, Lula had the support of his two older brothers, Vavá and Frei Chico, who were resolute in their commitment to assist and protect their brother during these physical altercations.

Vavá, a few years later, rescued a co-worker whose hair had become entangled in a weaving machine. Although he saved her, she lost the use of one hand as a result. Vavá passed away only in 2019, and Lula, who was in prison, was not permitted to attend his own brother's funeral. However, we will delve into that part of the story later.

The ability to lead and address coexistence issues is crucial for a career in politics. Without a doubt, Luiz began embracing this path from a young age. Do leaders develop themselves or are they inevitably propelled down that road by those in need of guidance?

In the early 1960s, Lula's professional journey

began like many young individuals, as an office boy answering phones and fulfilling various tasks assigned by the storage company that employed him. However, a few months later, a small opportunity arose that would prove decisive for the future president of Brazil: a chance at a career as a metallurgy worker. It started as an internship, working as a mechanic's assistant, but in practice, he served as a cleaner responsible for collecting metal scraps discarded by the machines. Nonetheless, he received a salary, wore a uniform, and held a signed work card. There was also a detail that would change his entire life: the chance to enroll in a professional technical course. In Brazil, initiatives like SENAI aim to provide practical vocational training for workers.

Within a few months, Lula successfully passed the test and managed to balance his time as both a worker and a student in the training course for mechanical lathes. Mechanical turners are professionals tasked with operating machines that produce various parts. In this manner, within three years, Lula, who had not progressed past the initial years of basic education, obtained his first diploma.

For Lula, these years were the most significant of his life, as they marked the first time he felt like a citizen. It was his initial encounter with citizenship. Having a job, appropriate attire, three meals a day, and the opportunity to engage in sports during breaks made him feel part of something greater, organized, and civilized. The effects of this experience would shape the young man's understanding that citizenship is fundamentally a collective concept.

During this period, Lula became acquainted with

strikes. Brazil had not yet entered a military dictatorship, which would commence a few years later. Consequently, these strikes were relatively mild, devoid of the massacres that would occur in subsequent years and decades. However, for someone who had yet to become politically aware and was solely concerned with providing for his siblings and mother, the strike days were viewed as welcome respites and nothing more. The ability to go for a leisurely stroll or simply stay at home and do nothing was quite tempting and rewarding.

Strikes were commonplace in Brazil, a country experiencing industrial growth, yet its workers faced financial hardships and often endured terrible working conditions. Occasionally, the strikes succeeded in making their voices heard.

Lula then began attending some of these protests, some peaceful. However, over time, starting in the 1960s, violence became prevalent. In one protest, the owner of a factory shot a protester and was subsequently disarmed, beaten, and killed by the demonstrators. Unfortunately, violence is a widespread occurrence in Brazil.

Having worked at the Marte Screws Factory for four years, Lula realized he was being paid less than other employees in the same role. Mistakenly, he asked his boss for a raise and was promptly fired. While participating in strikes is a right, requesting a raise was considered an "abuse" that the Brazilian industry did not take kindly to.

Forced to work the night shift at a smaller metallurgical plant, Lula moved on. It was in this factory that he suffered an accident in 1964, resulting in the loss of his little finger. Worker safety was not a priority or concern for the industry in Brazil during the 1960s, considering the absence of safety devices on machines and the lack of attention due to fatigue.

The accident occurred due to a dangerous combination of factors: machines lacking safety devices and sleep deprivation. While attempting to retrieve a newly manufactured screw from a press, Lula's colleague, responsible for holding the lever to prevent the press from descending, fell asleep at the exact moment Lula reached for the screw. The press descended rapidly, crushing Lula's little finger.

The accident took place at 3 am, but the doctor did not arrive until early morning and transported him to the nearest hospital. It is unclear whether out of negligence or indifference towards someone of lower socioeconomic status, the doctor opted to amputate Lula's entire finger, an extreme measure that could have been avoided. Speculation arose in subsequent decades about the possibility of saving parts of the finger, but the irreversible procedure had already been performed. Lula, a worker, lathe operator, and metallurgist, was left with nine fingers.

He received a reasonable compensation, enabling him to purchase a small plot of land for future house construction. Additionally, he was able to buy furniture for the modest house his family had occupied for several years.

After a few weeks of recovery at home, Lula returned to night work but only remained for a few more months. During this period, he alternated between jobs, unable to stay in one position for more than a year. Factors contributing to this instability included impulsive acts of youth, such as missing shifts to spend time at the beach with friends, as well as the prejudice and harshness prevalent during the first military government and the impending economic crisis.

3

MILITARY REGIME

IT IS important to note the historical context of this period in Brazil. Like many Latin American countries, Brazil experienced a period of military dictatorship from 1964 until its eradication in 1986. Lula's personal and political development is closely intertwined with the military regime, which many courageous individuals defiantly confronted.

The Brazilian military dictatorship resulted in the exile, arrest, torture, and death of thousands of people, displaying a complete lack of mercy and compassion. It is crucial to emphasize this fact because both the world and Brazil appear to have forgotten the atrocities committed by the extreme right when in power. As time has passed since the end of World War II, the memory of the millions of lives lost and the genocide has faded into a dangerously distant recollection.

In Brazil, we endured four years of a theocratic government with militaristic and extreme right leanings, which plunged the country into economic and health chaos. Brazil witnessed the highest number of COVID-19 deaths proportionally due to the denialist and corrupt practices of the government. Additionally, there was a cultural setback, with the dissolution of the Ministry of Culture in favor of militaristic agendas, and the hypocrisy of far-right churches.

Although these four years have come to an end, their repercussions will be felt for many years to come. These consequences range from increased poverty to the rise of domestic terrorism by those dissatisfied with the defeat of former President Bolsonaro in the elections. The shameful episode that occurred on January 8, 2023, when thousands of terrorists supporting the former president stormed Brasília and destroyed the headquarters of the three democratic powers, will forever stain Brazil's history.

This turbulent period connects to the history of Lula and the military dictatorship. Lula, who was elected in 2022, is the president who began to guide Brazil out of the abyss of denialism, death, and despair. While he may not transform the country into a paradise, he is undoubtedly the president who will initiate the process of rescuing Brazil from its present state of turmoil.

It is essential for every citizen of the world to be aware of and remember history so that we do not repeat its mistakes, as Edmund Burke famously stated. Lula's political engagement coincided with the onset of the military dictatorship, and although they were on opposite sides, their histories became intertwined. In 1964, Luiz, as a young man, faced even more challenges as he found himself unemployed after several years. Despite the added responsibilities, he had some money, mainly from the compensation he received, which allowed him to occasionally indulge in walks on the beach when he should have been working. Labor relations in Brazil have always been difficult, but in the 1960s, they were particularly dire and only worsened over time.

In March 1964, when the military staged a coup and ousted president-elect João Goulart, Lula found himself without a job. Unfortunately, the timing couldn't have been worse. The economy was set to contract in the following years, resulting in a scarce supply of jobs.

For the general public, who relied heavily on print and radio media, the events that transpired were not seen as a military coup but rather a democratic revolution. The narrative presented was that the military heroes had successfully eradicated the communist threat from the country. All newspapers supported the coup.

This situation bears some resemblance to the current rise of fascism in Brazil. While certain press outlets were committed to uncovering the truth, exposing the crimes and absurdities committed during Bolsonaro's fascist government over the course of four years, the average Brazilian, influenced by the misinformation spread on social networks, sees communism as a nonexistent, yet feared, entity. It is akin to the Boogeyman for innocent children.

At the age of 18, Lula naively believed that the army could solve Brazil's problems, despite being unaware of what those problems were and how an institution lacking expertise should never hold governmental powers.

In Brazil, there is a saying that goes: "When the pain is in the pocket, the eyes open." With time, after months of tirelessly searching for employment, Lula began to realize that not only were the military unable to solve Brazil's problems, but it seemed as though the situation was deteriorating. Lula would leave his house at six in the morning and walk 20 kilometers, visiting one factory after another in search of a job, only to return home barefoot with his swollen feet and a mind filled with frustration.

What made it even more disheartening was that Lula was well-qualified for a job, having completed a technical course. Yet, his chances were no greater than the masses who lacked professional training.

After eight months of daily treks, sweat, and tears of failure, Lula finally secured a job at the renowned Villares Factory. The factory specialized in manufacturing transatlantic engines, subway cars, and other transportation technologies. The Villares family, who owned the factory, boasted a prestigious lineage that included one of Brazil's greatest individuals in history, Santos Dumont, the true inventor of the airplane.

In the factory that produced towering 10-meter engines and other advanced technological products, Lula would spend the next decade. He had a signed work card, reasonable working conditions, and took great pride in securing this job through his own efforts.

As months went by, Lula's wages went straight towards addressing his family's numerous uncertainties. Dona Lindu, Lula's mother, had a simple yet effective system that would later inspire her son during his presidency. She pooled together the wages and informal earnings of all her children and herself, paid all the household and children's expenses, and then divided whatever was left equally among everyone, including herself.

This practical system of fair income distribution shed light on the future president's inclinations. Egalitarian distribution is not typically associated with right-wing ideologies, which are often rooted in natural inequalities. The survival system employed by an illiterate housewife who single-handedly raised a brood of children proved to be more effective than any Ph.D. could argue.

Lula's older brother earned a curious nickname: Frei Chico, due to a bald spot on a specific region of his head. He was the only politically conscious member of the family until that point, and since the 1964 military coup, he had also become a union member. The wanted posters plastered across Brazil by the military police, featuring images of "terrorists," were typically of trade unionists who fought for improved working conditions and, naturally, against the dictatorship.

However, Lula did not see it that way. In his eyes, criminals were the ones depicted on those posters, and so most people carried on with their lives, accepting and believing in the military government.

Friar Chico persistently urged Lula to attend a union meeting, but he always replied with a resounding "no." Lula enjoyed his work and playing football until exhaustion on weekends.

He let some opportunities pass in the name of his passion for football until love unexpectedly struck. He fell head over heels and, within a few months, became engaged to Lourdes, the sister of his best friend, who was affectionately known as Lambari, a type of Brazilian fish.

Between work, politics, and his blossoming relationship, the future president had no time to fight for a cause he believed didn't even exist.

And then, another wave of layoffs hit. Thousands of workers were dismissed across the industrial region of ABC. Lula managed to escape this round, but his more experienced brother had been let go.

It was Luiz's older brother's affiliation with unions that ultimately led him down this winding path, in a way that seemed natural. Lula, who worked in one of Brazil's largest factories, was presented with an opportunity to join the board of the union his brother Friar Chico belonged to. Despite not being politically inclined and initially believing that union members were all terrorists, Chico immediately recommended his brother for the position. After numerous conversations and meetings, Lula was convinced that he could take on an alternate vacancy, which didn't offer any compensation or legal protection against dismissal due to union activities. His fiancée, who had previously insisted on not marrying him while he held a director position, was satisfied with the alternate role and agreed to marry him as soon as possible. And so, Luiz Inácio soon found himself both married and a member of the union.

4

____

MARRIED MAN

For their honeymoon, Lula and his wife spent a week in Poços de Caldas, a tourist town in the state of Minas Gerais, Brazil. It was their first time enjoying a week-long vacation together, exploring the sights, going on dates, and indulging in the pleasures of life.

Upon their return, they settled into a modest dormitory, starting their simple yet fulfilling married life. However, work quickly called back the lathe operator who would eventually become the president of the republic.

With a more stable personal life, some money in his pocket, and food on the table, Lula began to look beyond himself. It's challenging to ask someone living in poverty or misery to see beyond their immediate needs.

As a substitute for the union's director, Paulo Vidal, Luiz's life began to change, along with the lives of workers in São Paulo's ABC region, and consequently, the industrial landscape of Brazil. Vidal, who was neither left nor right politically aligned, focused on the welfare of workers and advocating for their rights and responsibilities. This simple approach was enough to improve the quality of life for thousands of unionized workers. The workers' political awareness began to shift, and over the course of ten years, the percentage of unionized workers in São Paulo increased from 20% to over 50%.

Lula found himself missing barbecues and soccer games. When he wasn't working or resting at home, he could be found attending union meetings, supporting workers in their legal battles, and personally encouraging them to pursue professional training.

As a lathe operator, Lula was considered part of the working elite, enjoying higher wages and better working conditions. Through his influence, many individuals were able to take advantage of professional development opportunities, thanks to technical training programs.

A few decades later, millions of people would come to embrace this idea when Lula became president. During his first two terms, the number of university students surged from 8 million to 15 million.

Although initially an alternate, Lula gradually assumed additional responsibilities, surpassing his symbolic position. The labor union began offering educational and recreational opportunities to its members. As an extension of this initiative, the union also provided educational courses and lectures on Brazilian politics, economics, and related subjects.

As the workers became more politically engaged, the dictatorial government, which had suppressed numerous unions since 1964, began closely monitoring the metallurgist union with obvious curiosity. At the age of 23, Lula was fully immersed in the union and his marriage.

When it came to public speaking, however, Lula shied away from the microphone, avoiding it like the devil avoids the cross. Despite his lack of oratory skills, he devised a technique where he spoke to newspaper pictures of random people, effectively easing his extreme shyness. This technique helped prepare him for the future, where he would become one of the most accomplished orators in the political history of Brazil.

During his unjust imprisonment in Curitiba, a city in the south of the country, Lula continued to employ this technique. He used newspaper pictures as an outlet for conversation during the 580 days he spent in his individual cell.

But let's backtrack for a moment...

While pregnant, Lourdes never ceased to take on odd jobs to supplement her income. Even when she began experiencing severe stomach pains, she missed her appointments to earn some extra money.

However, the pain eventually became unbearable, and they rushed to the hospital. After being hospitalized for a few days, Lourdes lost the baby. When Lula arrived at the hospital, he already knew about the baby's death, but he received the devastating news that his first wife and first love had also passed away.

Grief is a peculiar and inevitable experience, with each person handling it in their own unique way. In Lula's case, he sought solace in his mother's house, isolating himself in her room for several months. Despite his personal mourning, he had no choice but to continue working. The mourning of the poor occurs during their limited spare time, and during those moments, Lula was alone. However, unlike many others, he did not resort to alcohol as a coping mechanism, a common crutch for Brazilians in general, not just those in mourning.

As the months passed, football and unionism gradually reintegrated him into social life. However, the process was slow and never fully overcome.

In 1972, a closely contested election between two unionist slates, the green and the blue, propelled Lula further on his journey toward the presidency of the country. Assuming the role of first secretary on the winning ticket, which was the second most important position, Lula became fully immersed in his union responsibilities. He took charge of social security matters and other crucial bureaucratic tasks aimed at safeguarding workers' rights. With his years of experience and transition from deputy to first secretary, Lula's name gained national recognition.

While director Vidal was unable to travel across the country, Luiz Inácio represented him and initiated the consolidation of a movement known at the time as the "new union wave in Brazil." This movement gained momentum as other regions and states began to align with the already influential ABC region of São Paulo.

During this time, Lula's actions garnered attention

not only from workers who appreciated his dedication but also from the communist party, which sought to recruit him. Lula's older brother, Frei Chico, a party member, attempted to mediate these discussions. However, Lula firmly rejected any association, not out of anti-communist sentiment, but because he believed it would compromise his integrity and dilute his strength in fighting against exploitative factories and for the rights of workers.

Lula was never a communist, neither before nor during his two previous presidential terms, and now, in his third term as the president of the republic.

Amidst the influence of anarchist ideologies from Italy, the limited impact of the Communist Party of Brazil (the country's first political party), and center-left positions, Lula's sole focus was on improving wages. This cause united people from diverse backgrounds, and it became Lula's unwavering fight.

A newly formed group of economists discovered that the federal government was manipulating inflation numbers, deliberately providing significantly lower figures than the actual data. This revelation made the unions realize that the battle ahead would be much more challenging than anticipated. Until then, confrontations between unions and a few arrests seemed relatively minor compared to the physical and psychological violence perpetrated by military governments.

Nonetheless, the unions and workers were determined to be prepared for whatever challenges lay ahead.

Meanwhile, in the blending of personal and professional life, as it naturally occurs, the division between these aspects of a human being, often emphasized in documentaries or tarot readings, becomes inconsequential in reality. In actuality, they are interconnected, forming an integral part of an individual's existence.

5

———

AFTER MOURNING

LULA, after a year of profound mourning, overcame his former shyness and began dating individuals from all walks of life. The ramifications of this would echo for many years, as one of his former girlfriends, whom he had supposedly betrayed, stepped forward during his initial presidential campaign to accuse him of pressuring her to terminate their pregnancies. However, none of these allegations were substantiated, but the murky and tumultuous moments in one's personal life always leave their mark.

During this time, Lula would meet, date, and eventually marry Marisa, who became his emotional anchor and lifelong companion. This served as preparation for the challenges that lay ahead, as one particular incident would profoundly impact Luiz and shed light on a recurring issue in Brazil - the dire lack of housing for millions of people.

As a young metallurgist, Lula and his newlywed wife purchased a modest home. However, upon visiting their new property, they discovered a dozen individuals already occupying the premises. Homelessness in Brazil has long been a pressing problem, and it has only worsened in recent years, affecting millions of people.

Despite presenting the necessary documentation, Lula failed to convince the occupants to vacate the property peacefully. Coercion became necessary, but witnessing such a disheartening scene made him realize that Brazil's problems ran far deeper than the propaganda perpetuated by the dictatorship, which controlled all radio and television stations.

The first year of their marriage went smoothly. Lula thrived in his employment and gained prestige as the first secretary in the labor union, where he exerted his influence and acted with determination, as was his nature. However, the turning point came in 1975, when due to various political factors, he was appointed as the leader of the ticket in the union elections, which he subsequently won.

On that occasion, Lula relied on a colleague to hold the microphone as he read his first pre-written speech. Over time and through extensive practice, as mentioned earlier, Lula would evolve into a formidable orator. However, that night was not his moment to shine.

Through a convoluted political maneuver, the state governor managed to persuade President Ernesto Geisel, the fourth president of the military regime, that Lula had triumphed over the communist party. As a result, Lula was granted a temporary respite from the oppressive gaze and control of the dictatorship, at least for the foreseeable future.

And in that same year, the future president embarked on a journey to Tokyo, where thousands of trade unionists convened at a congress sponsored by Toyota and Nissan. However, the trip proved to be fraught with complications. Lula fell ill, rendering him speechless, and faced another significant setback when his older brother, known as Frei Chico, a source of inspiration and a true affiliate of the Communist Party of Brazil, was abducted by the military police and subjected to torture.

Despite being forewarned of potential arrest and advised against returning to Brazil, Lula disregarded the warnings and immediately made his way back home. Upon his arrival, he spent the weekend feigning normalcy, hoping to determine if he was under surveillance by the authorities. Perhaps due to the information relayed to President Geisel, no immediate action was taken against him.

After a few days, Lula began his search for his brother, who had vanished for several days following his abduction by the police. The kidnapping involved armed individuals who blindfolded Frei Chico and escorted him to the dreaded Doi-Codi headquarters, one of the most notorious torture centers in Brazil's history.

Throughout its twenty-two-year existence, the military dictatorship left a trail of political arrests, torture, and even genocide against indigenous populations. It is no surprise that Colonel Carlos Brilhante Ustra, the cruelest torturer in Brazilian history, was not only mentioned but also honored by then-deputy Bolsonaro during the coup period that ousted President Dilma Rousseff. Years later, as president, Bolsonaro continued to advocate for torture, employed Nazi theories to address the pandemic, and engaged in the genocide of indigenous communities, along with numerous other crimes.

The true character of an individual is revealed by the figures they idolize.

Frei Chico endured fifteen days of torment at Doi-Codi. Under mounting societal pressure, the president began promising a gradual relaxation of repression and a return to civilian governance in the future. Such empty pledges had been heard since the 1964 coup; however, they began to take root, intensifying the pressure on the government. Nonetheless, the military extreme right, known as the ultra-right, still maintained control over certain government sectors. Doi-Codi was one such space, and Lula's brother experienced the full extent of this extremism. During his fifteen-day imprisonment, he endured merciless torture, spending sixteen hours a day in a chair with metal arms, infamously known as the "queen's armchair." Electrical wires connected to the chair delivered excruciating shocks, tearing his tongue and causing his teeth to grind as he lost control of his body, including his jaw. To exacerbate the suffering, the military personnel doused him with water and filled his mouth with salt.

Those who flirt with the extreme right nowadays are oblivious to the horrors endured by these individuals.

Even children were not spared from the cruelty of this inhumane regime.

After enduring two weeks of shocks and beatings,

Frei Chico was transferred to a different prison with a more moderate level of control. There, he was spared from torture. He spent a few more weeks in captivity before eventually being released. However, despite his freedom, hundreds of other political prisoners remained unjustly incarcerated, enduring unimaginable torture.

During this critical juncture in history, marked by the rise of Lula's popularity, as well as the heinous acts committed by the military dictatorship and the solidarity among intellectuals and students, the ideal conditions were created for the formation of a political party that would shape Luiz Inácio's life and, subsequently, the entire country: the Workers' Party, commonly known as the PT.

However, prior to the realization of this pivotal moment, the country experienced a wave of strikes, with the ABC region of São Paulo, led by Lula, at the forefront. In 1978, these strikes became increasingly frequent and intense, coinciding with the end of the repressive Institutional Act Number 5 (AI-5).

Under the AI-5 regime, which was established in 1968, any individual participating in strikes could face arrest, torture, and even death. AI-5 was one of the 17 institutional acts enforced by the military dictatorship in Brazil. Its implementation led to the closure of the National Congress and legislative assemblies across the states. Additionally, it allowed for the annulment of more than 170 legislative mandates, introduced prior censorship of the press and artistic productions, and granted the president the power to intervene in states and municipalities.

With AI-5 in effect, political gatherings unauthorized by the police became illegal, and curfews were imposed with increasing frequency. The regime remained in place for a decade, normalizing torture, murder, persecution, and gross violations of human rights under the military rule.

Signed on December 13, 1968, AI-5 formalized the targeted political persecution of the regime's opponents and authorized a series of extraordinary measures. These measures included the closure of the National Congress, intervention in states and municipalities, and the suspension of political rights for any citizen. Over 170 parliamentary mandates were nullified during this period, further consolidating the regime's control.

AI-5, the fifth institutional act enforced by the military dictatorship in Brazil, resulted in the suspension of individual rights and public freedoms, effectively eliminating any form of social control or participation by the State. This process of centralization and concentration of power in the hands of the military gradually intensified after the 1964 coup, reaching its peak in 1968.

The military takeover was a response to the progressive advancements made under the government of President João Goulart, who was ousted in 1964, as well as the cultural changes taking place in society. On the other hand, AI-5 was specifically established to suppress the organization of armed resistance and student mobilizations that began to gain momentum in 1966 and spread to other sectors of society. For instance, the March of the hundred thousand in 1968 brought together popular figures and artists who stood against the regime.

AI-5 was an attempt to tighten control precisely because the dictatorship felt it was losing its grip on society and failing to maintain a facade of normalcy. Following the enactment of AI-5, there was a decline in these movements, interrupting the mobilization process that had been unfolding in previous years.

Subsequently, the dictatorship's surveillance and espionage apparatus operated more freely, with little possibility of judicial oversight to prevent abuses and violations of human rights committed by the military.

One of the most egregious violations permitted by AI-5 was the suspension of habeas corpus, a legal safeguard ensuring that individuals accused of crimes are not unlawfully deprived of their freedom or subjected to violence, coercion, or abuse of power.

The military dictatorship led Brazil to deviate significantly from the standards outlined in the Universal Declaration of Human Rights, which celebrated its 70th anniversary last Monday (10th). AI-5 materialized the extensive human rights violations that the dictatorship would carry out in the years to come.

When President Geisel eventually ended the AI-5, Lula and the unions were prepared to make up for lost time and fight for their rights, which had been suppressed and suppressed for many years, even predating the dictatorship.

This period saw the occurrence of numerous strikes, with the majority receiving support from all levels of factory hierarchy, from directors and managers to janitors.

The notable distinction during this era of what was called "new unionism" was that despite union support and Lula's influential leadership, the strikes originated from the factory workers themselves. These grassroots movements often have the most enduring and tangible impact on changes in labor rights.

6

A PARTY IS BORN

In the annals of history, the strikes that took place in massive factories like Scania are etched into memory, owing to their significant following numbering in the thousands.

As early as 1979, Lula managed to assemble a multitude of workers in a strike that encompassed numerous factories in the ABC region of São Paulo. This region accounted for approximately 10% of the country's industrial earnings. Addressing a crowd of over 30,000 workers in a stadium, their collective demand was for wage replacement.

However, the military dictatorship retaliated in response. Union leaders were ousted from their positions and replaced with individuals appointed by the military regime, often resorting to violent means.

Yet, the strikes persisted. Despite facing setbacks, attacks, and arrests, the year 1979 held promise for the rights of these workers who not only shaped the history of Brazil but the very essence of the nation itself.

The federal government's attempt to silence Lula by dismissing him from the union backfired. Lula secretly continued to lead the union, and his subsequent gathering attracted a staggering 70,000 attendees. On May 1st, a grand march with 150,000 participants flooded the streets, and the government's efforts proved futile against the strength of the people.

From Lula's own mind emerged the concept of a 45-day truce, during which workers would resume their normal duties while awaiting the jointly requested salary adjustments. If these adjustments were not met, the strike would reignite after the specified period.

And on May 12, 1979, the strikers attained their desired wage increase. Although smaller in magnitude than their initial demands, this victory carried significant weight. Yet, beyond the monetary readjustments, a sense of popular strength emerged, empowering the workers to vociferously advocate for their rights in the years to come.

Prior to the establishment of the PT (Workers' Party), Brazil witnessed the formation of its first workers' party in this new political era. The Workers' Party of Brazil, created in 1945 by then-president Getúlio Vargas, held the distinction of being the first. Subsequently, the Democratic Labor Party (PDT) arose in 1979 from a gathering of Brazilian labor representatives and those in exile, under the leadership of Leonel Brizola. This assembly took place in Portugal, with the esteemed presence of Portuguese leader Mário Soares, and resulted in the approval of the Charter of Lisbon, which laid the groundwork for the new party.

The intention was to rescue the acronym PTB (Brazilian Labor Party), but a legal maneuver backed by the military government ultimately placed it in the hands of politicians deemed "subservient to power" - as described by Brizola, who had returned to Brazil after 15 years in exile.

In May 1980, the historic Labor Party held multiple meetings and approved its program, manifesto, and statutes, declaring its commitment to the defense of nationalism and democratic socialism. Notable pillars included education, with a focus on the well-being of children and young people in Brazil, as well as the protection of workers' interests.

Consequently, the party began to establish its presence nationwide, starting primarily in Rio de Janeiro and Rio Grande do Sul. And in the first democratic election following the military regime in 1982, the PDT successfully elected Leonel Brizola as the governor of Rio de Janeiro. Additionally, two senators and 24 federal deputies were elected. Brizola later ran in the 1989 presidential elections and subsequently returned to govern Rio de Janeiro.

In 1980, the Workers' Party emerged, driven by the aspirations of union leaders, intellectuals, artists, religious activists, and political advocates who had endured years of exile and persecution under the military dictatorship. They united to form an organizational party that would champion the interests and struggles of the Brazilian working class. Concurrently, a new form of combative and independent unionism emerged in the country, culminating in the establishment of the CUT (Unified Workers' Central) and other class entities.

The PT, or Workers' Party, was founded through a significant alliance between trade unionists, intellectuals, artists, sectors connected to Liberation Theology within the Catholic Church, and political militants who opposed the military dictatorship and returned to the country following the enactment of amnesty.

Following the major strikes organized by the trade union movement in the ABC region of São Paulo in 1979 and 1980, trade unionists led by Luiz Inácio Lula da Silva recognized the imperative to create a political party within the process of the country's democratization. This party would actively defend the struggles of the Brazilian working class and participate in their organization.

This objective is explicitly stated in the text of the PT Program, which was approved during the party's formation process:

"(...) The PT was born in a context in which democracy emerges as one of the prominent issues in Brazilian society. For the PT, the current concrete struggle for democracy is to ensure the workers' right to organize freely at all levels. Therefore, the democracy that workers propose holds enduring value, one that rejects the economic exploitation and marginalization of the millions of Brazilians who contribute to the country's wealth through their labor (...)."

On February 10, 1980, at Colégio Sion in São Paulo, the Workers' Party Manifesto was launched, with the participation of trade unionists, intellectuals, artists, and Catholics associated with Liberation

Theology. The document was later published in the Official Gazette on October 21 of the same year.

"The Workers' Party emerges from the millions of Brazilians' need to intervene in the country's social and political life in order to transform it. The most important lesson Brazilian workers have learned from their struggles is that democracy is a conquest that must be built by their own hands," states the opening passage of the manifesto.

Legendary political activist Apolônio de Carvalho signs Membership Form Number 1, followed by art critic Mário Pedrosa, literary critic Antonio Candido, and historian and journalist Sérgio Buarque de Hollanda, who were prominent figures in the Brazilian intellectual scene and the democratic struggle during the military dictatorship.

As expected, the prominent union leader and main architect of the party's construction, Luiz Inácio Lula da Silva, is elected as president of the first Provisional National Executive Committee of the party.

The alliance between union leaders and political militants from the former Brazilian left, who had fought against the military regime and regained their political rights during the political opening process, allowed for a broad debate on the party's ideological proposal. From its inception, the PT made the ideological choice for democratic socialism, criticizing the socialist models implemented in other countries at that time, as well as the reformism proposed by the social-democratic parties.

During the 1st National Meeting held on August 8 and 9, 1981, the Internal Regulations were approved and the members of the first National Board were elected, with Lula as the national president.

Simultaneously with the creation of the PT, union leaders in various regions of the country began the reorganization of a union movement independent of state control, which was prevalent during the Vargas Era. This culminated in the Conference of the Working Classes (CONCLAT) on August 21, 1981, leading to the establishment of the Single Workers' Central (CUT).

On February 11, 1982, the PT officially received recognition as a political party from the Superior Electoral Court (TSE).

Following its official recognition by the TSE, the PT participated in its first elections in 1982 and successfully elected trade unionist Gilson Menezes as its first mayor in Diadema, located in the Greater ABC region of São Paulo.

In 1984, the party's leaders and members mobilized nationwide in the historic struggle for "Diretas Já" (Direct Elections), playing a fundamental role in reigniting the Brazilian people's hope for building a democratic, fair, and egalitarian society - principles that have always guided the foundation and existence of the PT.

In 1988, the PT achieved an influential presence in the National Constituent Assembly, which was responsible for discussing, formulating, and approving a new Constitution for the country. Throughout the deliberation process, the PT's experience in advocating for social demands served as the basis for numerous proposals presented in the 1988 Constituent

Assembly. These proposals ultimately led to the approval of the current Brazilian constitution. The PT, along with other leftist parties, made significant advancements in terms of social rights and the democratization of various public policies.

7

STRIKING TOWARDS DEMOCRACY

In 1989, after 29 years of authoritarianism and political terror, Brazil held presidential elections once again. The PT conducted a historic campaign driven by emotion and the desire for social transformation, led by its prominent leader, Lula. Despite facing formidable financial and media powers dominating the national scene, Lula reached the second round. However, the PT faced the first of many hate campaigns characterized by slander and defamation, which would shape the party's trajectory. Ultimately, Lula was defeated.

Nonetheless, from that point onward, the PT solidified its position, assuming a vanguard role in the Brazilian political landscape. The party actively participated in major national movements and electoral processes, establishing itself as a significant national and international political force. Today, it is recognized as the largest and most influential left-wing party in Latin America.

After experiencing defeats in the presidential

elections of 1994 and 1998, the PT achieved victory in the presidency with Lula in 2002. Lula was re-elected in 2006, and the party secured further wins with Dilma Rousseff in 2010 and 2014, resulting in nearly 14 years of governance prioritizing social justice, economic growth, and equal rights in the exercise of citizenship.

Throughout its more than four decades of existence, the PT has actively engaged in national political life, both through municipal and state administrations and on a national level. The party's presence in parliamentary bodies and the three branches of government has allowed it to implement the "PT Mode," which has become a historical reference in Brazilian politics.

Returning to the party's formation in 1980, the truth is that the idea of a workers' party originated from the dissatisfaction felt by Lula and his colleagues in witnessing the lack of representation for workers in the national congress. Lula and his comrades in the ABC region had contemplated for months the idea of establishing a political party rooted in the working class.

In the beginning, astonishment arose due to the nearly complete absence of workers among congressmen. The realization that there were only two workers among almost five hundred federal senators and deputies left Lula with a sense of unease. This issue became a recurring topic in all the debates, meetings, and congresses in which he participated. Whenever he was invited to discuss salary issues, inflation, or unemployment, he would cautiously navigate the subject until he finally addressed the root cause: a significant portion of the responsibility for the poverty experienced by poor Brazilians lay in the lack of representation of workers in the legislative chambers, where laws governing the entire country were made.

Lula's transformation, marked by his public aversion to politics and those who engaged in it, began to surface during the congress of oil workers in mid-1978 in Bahia. This transformation reemerged in January 1979 in the city of Lins, located in the interior of São Paulo, during the 9th Congress of Metallurgical, Mechanical, and Electrical Material Workers of the State of São Paulo.

Although Lins was not an industrial center, it was chosen as the venue because its mayor, Waldemar Casadei, belonged to the "authentic" faction of the opposition party to the military regime, known as the MDB. In addition to bringing the discussion of the creation of a workers' party to the forefront, the meeting in Lins allowed the press and public opinion access to information that had previously only circulated within union circles: the broad support for Lula from various left-leaning groups.

The Workers' Party was established not as a socialist party, but as a party representing the interests of workers. Senator and future President of the Republic, Fernando Henrique Cardoso, who had a complicated relationship with Lula at the time, disapproved of the non-socialist direction of the party's formation, as did many other more leftist factions.

Officially established in February 1980, although its official registration was only published in October and April, the party faced further challenges as Lula led another strike, resulting in his arrest, along with numerous union leaders.

Despite this setback, the party was founded, and the course of Brazilian history would be forever altered.

When apprehended, along with the entire union board, Lula remained composed, as he had already prepared for the possibility of arrest. The unions had more than a hundred coordinators, ready for such an event. Even with Lula's arrest and the detention of his colleagues, the strikes persisted, with meetings and assemblies proceeding as usual.

All detainees endured harsh interrogations, with psychological torture and lengthy questioning taking a toll on everyone, particularly Luiz, who spent over four hours answering a wide range of questions, from the deeply personal to the far-fetched. However, it was through these interrogations that the military government concluded that Lula was not a communist, nor was he associated with any clandestine or dangerous movements, according to the conservative military perspective.

The massive strike persisted on the streets, now met with forceful action from the army. Violence permeated the protests, always originating from the top down, with the military on horseback wielding batons against the workers.

Lula had been imprisoned for over two weeks, and his mother, Lindu, was battling cancer. Romeu Tuma, the delegate in charge of the political repression unit that had apprehended Lula and his colleagues, found a covert way to facilitate Lula's visit to his ailing mother.

Even during the dictatorship, Lula managed to see his mother, despite being incarcerated. However, in 2019, despite having a release order from the Federal Supreme Court of Brazil, Lula was only permitted to attend the funeral of his brother, Vavá, if he was transported to the state where he was imprisoned, within a military institution. This decision was made by Sérgio Moro, the man responsible for Lula's unjust conviction and a close ally of the fascist president Jair Bolsonaro. Jurists from around the world criticized Moro's actions as degrading and inhumane, accusing him of serving a fascist agenda.

Looking back, during the two-hour visit with his mother, Lula tried to console her by assuring her that he was being treated well by the police and expressing his wishes for her recovery. As daybreak approached, the car returned to the police station's underground garage, and Lula was returned to his cell.

On the 21st day of his arrest, lawyer Luiz Eduardo Greenhalgh emerged from the Department of Politics and Social Order (Dops), responsible for political repression and prisons, after visiting the prisoners. He announced to reporters that his clients had declared a hunger strike. However, there was no unanimity among the prisoners regarding the strike, including Lula himself, who initially opposed this form of protest. Eventually, Lula agreed, recognizing the limited avenues for communication while in custody. Lula personally conveyed the decision to delegate Romeu Tuma, who reacted angrily but did not follow through with his threats to restrict the prisoners' access to radios, soccer, sunbathing, and newspapers.

Three days later, while visiting his clients,

Greenhalgh heard Lula express his desire to put an end to the hunger strike. Lula's friend caught him attempting to break the strike by unwrapping hidden sweets under his pillow. Later that day, to everyone's relief, they received a message from Bishop Cláudio Hummes urging an end to the protest in the name of God.

Displaying an unexpected sense of humor, the director of Dops, Armando Panichi, personally instructed investigators to purchase a plate of fried squid from the Greek restaurant Acropolis to feed the starving prisoners. Meanwhile, Tuma celebrated news from ABC, as an assembly had ended the strike after 41 days without any concessions for the workers.

For Lula, the bad news continued to pile up. On May 12th, at eleven o'clock in the morning, word reached the Dops jail that Dona Lindu had passed away. Once again, the director of Dops summoned investigators to accompany Lula to two funeral arrangements: the first being the wake at the "Beneficência Portuguesa Hospital of São Caetano do Sul," where Lindu had been hospitalized.

It was not an unexpected death. Lula knew that his mother's health was very precarious, and the cancer was advancing through the 64-year-old woman's body. But the son was losing the person he had been and would forever remain his reference in life. For him, there was no doubt that his own characteristics, such as obstinacy, a sense of decency, and the ability to face obstacles, were clear inheritances from his mother. Even after being elected President of the Republic, Lula would never tire of repeating that his mother was an example for everything in his character.

He spent fifty minutes in tears with his wife, Marisa, beside the body. On his way back to the DOPS, suffering from a severe toothache, the police took him to a dental office to have his wisdom tooth extracted.

The second task of the two investigators would be completed at half-past nine the following morning: to take Lula to Lindu's burial in the Vila Pauliceia cemetery on Júlio de Mesquita street in São Bernardo do Campo. The ceremony nearly turned into a political demonstration, which even worried police officer Panichi. "There were only two of us, and on Tuma's orders, we were unarmed. What about the people, for God's sake? A crowd of at least 3 thousand people. He could barely walk. The crowd shouted, 'Free Lula!' I didn't move a meter away from him the whole time. Leaving was very difficult. If I hadn't grabbed his boy, Fábio, and thrown him into the car through the window, I think he would have been crushed. We left with Lula, his wife, and the boy. We tried to leave the cemetery through the back, but the gate was closed. The only way was to leave through the front gate, almost running over people."

Although the strike had already ended, Lula and his companions remained in prison as they were covered by the National Security Law. On the 14th, former governor Leonel Brizola, who had returned to Brazil months before, was prevented from entering the Dops as the incommunicado ban was still in effect. They all stayed at the Dops until May 20 when Greenhalgh was informed by the Military Justice that the arrests had been revoked. Panichi was given the mission to take Lula in a beige "Veraneio" van with a cold plate to the vicinity of his home in São Bernardo, where a crowd of workers, politicians, and lawyers was already waiting for him.

Upon entering the house, he embraced his wife and children, went to the backyard, and made a gesture full of symbolism and meaning. He opened the cage and released the anu, a black singing bird that he had been raising for many years.

In a few weeks, all of Lula's unionist colleagues would be free, but like Luiz, they were all fired. It is important to remember that from that time until today, one or two months without a salary is enough to make a Brazilian family starve. The great financial difficulties mean that Brazilians, in general, do not have the right to be without a job even for a month.

In this manner, the individuals who were dismissed came together and established a small business. However, they relied on investments to purchase industrial equipment, which, even if modest, always came at a high cost. Assistance was provided by unionist friends from Sweden, but primarily from Chico Buarque de Holanda, one of the greatest singers and composers of Brazilian popular music, and a dedicated activist. Chico Buarque de Holanda was also one of the exiles forced out by the military regime.

Two months after being released, Lula found himself at the sweltering airport in Managua, the capital of Nicaragua, anxiously awaiting the arrival of Cuban President Fidel Castro, whose plane was scheduled to land in a matter of minutes.

That day marked the one-year anniversary of the

Sandinista National Liberation Front's victory, which had brought an end to the dictatorship of Anastasio Somoza, the heir to a family dynasty that had ruthlessly ruled the country, engaging in torture and looting since the 1930s.

Fidel had departed from Havana that morning, accompanied by a small delegation. It was Fidel's first time setting foot on Nicaraguan soil, and he had personally chosen to attend the celebration. Apart from supporting the Sandinista guerrilla struggle, the Cuban Revolution had numerous reasons to join in the festivities with their neighboring country. It was in Somoza-controlled Nicaragua that the CIA had trained a portion of the mercenaries who had attempted to invade Cuba in the disastrous and failed Bay of Pigs operation in April 1961. During that time, Somoza had personally bid farewell to the mercenary army, making a request to its members at the end of his speech: "After you take power, I don't want you to bring me a cent from Cuba. I just want a beard from the corpse of communist Fidel Castro."

Lula had left Brazil under the accusation of violating the National Security Law, a charge that would later result in him and his fellow prison inmates being sentenced to three and a half years in prison for their strikes at the beginning of the year.

Due to his ongoing legal proceedings, Lula was compelled to seek permission from military judge Nelson da Silva Machado Guimarães to leave the country. Judge Guimarães, in turn, ordered the DOPS (Department of Political and Social Order) to return Lula's passport and issue him an exit visa. (During the dictatorship, all Brazilians were required to obtain an "exit visa" from the authorities to travel abroad.)

Despite everything, Lula did not want to miss the opportunity to personally meet the legendary idol of a generation of young people worldwide, the bearded Fidel Castro, who had boldly established a communist regime just over a hundred kilometers away from the United States.

Lula was introduced to Fidel, marking the beginning of a friendship that endured until the Cuban leader's death in 2016. Lula would later participate in Fidel's funeral.

That night, following a lengthy formal conversation, Fidel extended an invitation to Lula to visit Cuba—a journey that would not take place until a few years later, but would ultimately have a profound impact on the Brazilian metallurgist's political future.

Upon returning to Brazil, Lula faced a grave predicament: a trial in the Military Court. Despite having the opportunity to employ renowned legal minds, such as the esteemed jurist Heleno Fragoso, Lula chose to entrust his defense to Greenhalgh, a young lawyer of only 32 years who lacked the expected professional experience for such a challenging and high-stakes case. This decision, akin to his later choice to rely on the relatively unknown Cristiano Zanin and Valeska Teixeira—spouse of his old friend Roberto Teixeira—in the infamous "Lava Jato" operation, turned out to be a testament to Lula's intuition.

Following the conclusion of the festivities in Managua, Lula returned to São Bernardo do Campo and wasted no time in attending a public event to launch the PT in the northern region of Brazil.

After the rally, Lula embarked on a 200-kilometer journey to the city of Brasiléia, located in the interior of the state of Acre, accompanied by Chico Mendes, a rubber tapper and environmentalist who had recently joined the Workers' Party. Tragically, nine years later, Mendes would fall victim to a fatal shooting orchestrated by farmers. Upon arriving in the small town of Brasiléia, situated on the border with Bolivia, Lula and Mendes immediately led a public protest in response to the recent murder of Wilson de Sousa Pinheiro, president of the local rural workers' union. The atmosphere was charged with emotion. According to a Federal Police report, which had agents present in the crowd, when Lula and Mendes took the stage, "approximately [...] thirty individuals had already spoken, with some expressing fiery sentiments and demanding revenge." The tension escalated further when Jaco, a speaker known for his impassioned rhetoric, addressed the audience. He declared, "Our land shall not be surrendered to foreigners or capitalists. It belongs to the people, and they shall conquer it, be it through sweat, blood, or whatever means necessary."

When Lula was given the opportunity to speak, the former president of the ABC union raised the level of radicalism in his tone. "Those responsible for Wilson's murder must have spies among us. Let it be known that the Brazilian working class is weary of empty promises, hunger, fleeing, and death," Lula proclaimed. The audience erupted in applause, and he continued, delivering a message that would later land him in legal trouble under the National Security Law for the second time in two months. "Bosses are worthless in São Paulo, worthless in Brasília, worthless in Rio de Janeiro, and worthless anywhere in the world. [...] All the boss desires is the worker's blood, sweat, and death. [...] But the time for change is approaching."

The day after the speeches, Nilo Sérgio de Oliveira, the alleged killer of Wilson Pinheiro and the foreman of a farm in Brasiléia, was surrounded, lynched, and killed by thirty men armed with revolvers, scythes, axes, shotguns, and rifles. According to the police, all the aggressors were members of the city's rural workers union. Lula and three other speakers at the event on Sunday night were accused of being the masterminds of the crime and framed under the National Security Law. In the petition filed by the president of the Agriculture Federation of Acre, Lula, Jacó, and the other five were accused of promoting "an apology for revenge, hatred, and inciting the large number of workers present to subvert the political-social order and engage in violence between the social classes. They succeeded in their criminal intent, which culminated in the death of landowner Nilo Sérgio de Oliveira."

Months later, the Military Prosecutor's Office for the North region of Brazil accepted the accusation and charged Lula, Jacó, and the other five, holding them responsible for the death of the farmer.

Contag (National Confederation of Agricultural Workers) hired Heleno Fragoso to defend the accused members of the organization. Greenhalgh, in charge of defending Lula and Jacó, invited a friend, José Paulo

Sepúlveda Pertence, a lawyer from Brasilia who would later become a minister and president of the Federal Supreme Court, to travel with him to Manaus, the capital of the state of Amazonas in northern Brazil, where the trial would take place.

Greenhalgh's defense, more than a law textbook, would fit into a story of magical realism by Gabriel García Márquez. The young lawyer from São Paulo embarked on a meticulous and detailed investigative work, collaborating with the unionists of Brasiléia, in order to find an explanation for a crucial question: how did they conclude that "Nilão" was responsible for Wilson Pinheiro's execution? All the answers pointed to a local belief known among farmers, miners, and workers in the region. One of the witnesses summarized it: "Doctor, before burying Wilson Pinheiro, we put a coin under his tongue. And we tie the face of the deceased with a cloth so that the mouth does not open and the coin doesn't come out. Everyone here knows that this method is infallible: if someone is killed and you put a coin under the dead man's tongue and close his mouth, the killer always returns to the grave site." Even in the face of the lawyer's astonishment, the rural worker continued with absolute naturalness: "We buried Wilson, everyone left, but we left a scout in the cemetery, hidden in a corner. When there was no one left, guess who appears and spends a long time looking at the grave? Nilo. He arrived, stayed there for half an hour in silence, spying on the place where Wilson had been buried. He didn't need anything else: it was him."

During his oral defense, Greenhalgh spent twelve hours at the Military Audit in Manaus, lasting throughout the night. The lawyer argued that Nilo's death did not result from Lula's and Jaco's speeches but from a popular belief that was well-known to everyone present, including judges, prosecutors, and the public. As the trial attracted significant attention, especially with Lula as the defendant, politicians and artists sympathetic to the PT could be identified in the audience, all with their eyes fixed on Greenhalgh.

In a lengthy exposition, he delved into the connection between superstitions and reality. He discussed the symbolism associated with various superstitions such as black cats, walking under stairs, crossing fingers, and Friday the 13th. However, it was when he reached the topic of a coin under a dead man's tongue that the lawyer, exhausted and overcome by the heat, fell into a victorious slumber, knowing that Lula and Jaco had been acquitted.

The decision of the Manaus Military Court brought relief to trade unionists, Lula's supporters, PT followers, and those who had participated in strikes. However, everyone was aware that there was another obstacle to overcome—the trial of the strikers scheduled for February 1981.

As the trial date approached for the union directors who had been impeached and falsely implicated under the National Security Act for their involvement in the strikes of the early 1980s, a high-risk plan orchestrated by Greenhalgh shuffled the cards of Military Justice. The hearing was set for Wednesday, February 25. On the morning of the preceding Friday, the 20th, the lawyer went to the

Audit building to obtain passwords for the prisoners' relatives. Located in a two-story house in São Paulo, the military division had a jury room that could accommodate just over forty people. As was typical for many public offices on Fridays, the place was deserted. Greenhalgh wandered from room to room in search of the clerk responsible for the passwords, but found nothing. It was then that he heard the sound of a typewriter as he passed by a room. Curiosity piqued, he entered and discovered an Army sergeant typing on sheets of paper adorned with the local crest. Peering over the soldier's shoulder, as if he had no ulterior motive, Greenhalgh stumbled upon a legal atrocity: five days before the trial, the sentences for the defendants were already being typed. The auditor judge, Nelson da Silva Machado Guimarães, would merely read the sentences, irrespective of the defense's arguments. With eyes wide open in disbelief, the lawyer began to read aloud what was typed:

"(...) As per Article 36, Item II of Law 6620/78, I hereby sentence the defendants to the following prison terms: Luiz Inácio da Silva, 3 years and 6 months; Enilson Simões de Moura, 3 years and 6 months; Djalma de Souza Bom, 3 years..." Before Greenhalgh could finish reading the entire list of defendants and their sentences, the sergeant hastily turned the sheet over, his face pale with terror. "You're not going to use that, are you, Doctor?" the sergeant pleaded. "If this becomes public, it will ruin my career..." Greenhalgh swiftly descended the stairs of the mansion, which would later be transformed into the Memorial of the Fight for Justice, and joined the defendants and the lawyers who were defending the trade unionists. He proposed a daring plan: in addition to exposing the plot to the public, the defendants and their lawyers should boycott the trial to denounce the farce orchestrated by the dictatorship to condemn Lula and his fellow union colleagues. The renowned lawyers were taken aback by this audacious suggestion, arguing that it was absurd and outrageous. They feared that it could result in the immediate arrest of all the accused on the grounds of disrespecting the military dictatorship's version of justice.

On the designated day, the judge commenced the session and waited for the appointed time. As neither the defendants nor their lawyers appeared, he appointed a dative lawyer named Paulo Rui de Godói, who requested an hour to review the records. At six o'clock in the evening, the verdict was delivered, with all defendants being sentenced in absentia. Just as Greenhalgh had predicted, Lula and several trade unionists were each sentenced to three and a half years in prison, while others received two-year sentences.

The lawyers filed appeals against the verdicts, which were subsequently confirmed by the judge. After numerous back-and-forths between the Military Audit of São Paulo and appeals to the Superior Military Court, all the sentences were eventually annulled. In April of that same year, following the end of the federal intervention in the São Paulo ABC union, Lula made the decision not to run for office.

What piqued general curiosity was Lula's fate: would he abandon his trade union activities for a political career with the creation of the PT? In a personal letter addressed to him shortly before the union's election, activist and theologian Frei Betto posed these questions, which interested not only the Dominican friar but the entire political class. Would you engage in politics? What prompted you to enter politics? Why form the party? Will you return to being a simple worker? Do you aspire to be a governor? I believe you have an excellent opportunity ahead of you to convey your message to the masses on the day you pass the union's leadership to your teammates on plate 1 (I am confident they will emerge victorious).

Those who were unaware of Lula's future plans remained in the dark. He vaguely hinted at his future in two obscure sentences during an interview with the newspaper O Estado de S. Paulo, stating, "I have no project for the future. My destiny is tied to my professional category." His daily routine reaffirmed this response. While overseeing the expansion of the PT nationwide, his efforts seemed focused on trade union work. This included the election of a new director and, most importantly, the arduous task of establishing a unified central workers' organization. This organization aimed to bring together not only manual laborers but also unionized professionals such as doctors, teachers, journalists, engineers, and others.

In between his travels across Brazil, Lula dedicated himself to expanding his international reach, often accompanied by university professors Francisco Weffort and José Álvaro Moisés. The latter had already been appointed as the PT's Secretary of International Relations. Of course, they were always under the watchful eye of the authorities.

During one of these international trips, Lula acquired two distinctive gadgets. For the PT, he brought a super-8 camcorder, as domestic VHS videos were still in their infancy in Brazil. This technology was utilized in campaigns to establish the party nationwide. For the union, he purchased a portable device known as a decibel meter, which measured noise levels. ABC union inspectors could use it to assess whether the ambient noise in factories complied with labor standards.

The creation of the trade union central proved to be more challenging than Lula had initially anticipated. Since the dictatorship extinguished the old CGT (General Workers' Command) in 1964, there had been no successful attempt to establish an organization that would unify the country's unions.

The necessity for a central organization became evident during the National Conference of the Working Class held in August 1981 in the state of São Paulo. Thousands of delegates from various unions across Brazil were present. Leaders from trade union centrals in West Germany, France, Venezuela, Portugal, Angola, Argentina, and the leader of the World Trade Union Front also attended. Accommodating and feeding this large crowd over the three-day event was costly, financed through union contributions, car raffles, and donations. A rough estimate revealed that the National Conference of the Working Class represented 12 million workers.

Despite the exemplary organization, the presence of numerous factions and political currents hindered an agreement on the creation of a single central. Two opposing chains clashed. One, led by trade unionists affiliated with the Communist Party of Brazil and represented by a metallurgist from Santos named

Arnaldo Gonçalves, advocated for a corporatist and centralized institution.

The other, with Lula at the helm, advocated for a grassroots-centered approach in the workplace that was more receptive to diverse influences. Ultimately, the Conference gave rise to not one, but two major trade union federations, namely the Central Única dos Trabalhadores (Unified Workers' Central or CUT), closely tied to the Partido dos Trabalhadores (Workers' Party or PT), and the Força Sindical (Union Strength), led by Jair Meneguelli and Luiz Antonio de Medeiros respectively. Medeiros, a former Communist Party militant, had already begun to embrace "Eurocommunism" and had distanced himself from the collapsing Soviet Union.

In addition to Lula's acquittals in the strike and Acre incidents, as well as the failed amnesty approval, the emergence of two union federations signaled that the days of the dictatorship were numbered. As Ulysses Guimarães, the leader of the opposition, aptly put it, they were facing a "toothless and vegetarian lion."

However, the true turning point towards the democratization of Brazil came on January 19, 1982, when General Figueiredo, the final dictator-president, called for direct, free, and secret elections to be held on November 15 of that year. These elections would encompass governors, vice-governors, senators, federal and state deputies, mayors, vice-mayors, and councilors.

The last direct elections for governors had taken place seventeen years earlier in 1965, and the military regime had suffered defeats in the major states of

Minas Gerais, Santa Catarina, Mato Grosso, and Rio de Janeiro (Guanabara).

To fully restore democracy and leave behind the remnants of authoritarian rule, the country now only needed direct elections for the President of the Republic, which would occur seven years later in 1989, following the National Constituent Assembly. However, the direct election of state governors was already a significant step forward.

In São Paulo, the Workers' Party placed all its hopes on an unbeatable candidate, Lula. Since votes were still manually recorded, the PT's first move was to officially change Lula's name from Luiz Inácio da Silva to Luiz Inácio Lula da Silva, ensuring that votes cast for "Lula" would not be invalidated.

This name change also affected Marisa, Lula's wife, and their four children, who all adopted the surname "Lula da Silva."

Yet, the lack of resources posed the biggest challenge for the campaign. Even in the party's birthplace, São Paulo, with its 571 municipalities, over 300 had no PT presence or candidate. While Lula's competitors traveled on chartered planes, he was limited to commercial flights, which often did not align with the campaign's needs. He frequently resorted to traveling by car. Furthermore, Lula's national prominence led him to prioritize supporting PT candidates for governor, senator, and deputy in various states across Brazil, always relying on commercial flights for transportation.

Everything was done on the fly. Marisa, who had taken a free silkscreen course, set up a workshop at home to print 22,000 t-shirts featuring the PT's star emblem, the party's most prominent symbol to this day. Lula's journeys throughout the state, sometimes to cities over 600 kilometers away from the capital, were undertaken by car. Lula would drive in a borrowed Volkswagen, with the campaign car behind him illuminating the road ahead as darkness fell, enabling him to read the speeches he would deliver in the next municipality. When no organized rally awaited them, Lula would stand on the running board of the VW Beetle, megaphone in hand, touring the city and conducting his own propaganda while inviting passers-by to join the PT.

One of the remnants of the authoritarian regime was the "Falcon Law," named after its author, Armando Falcão, who served as the Minister of Justice under Geisel. According to this law, electoral television programs featured only the candidate's photo, whether they were running for governor or councilor, along with a brief summary of their biography read by an announcer in a matter of seconds.

The PT campaigns aimed to appeal to and win over the working class, and after presenting each candidate's mini-biography, the announcer would proclaim, "A Brazilian just like you." Lula, lacking funds to hire research institutes, gauged his popularity by the number of people he could gather in public squares and rallies. As the press itself confirmed, his gatherings continued to attract more and more people, particularly in medium and large cities with factories, workers, universities, and students.

Among the youth, the success of the PT and Lula seemed indisputable, and the possibility of victory became increasingly plausible. The massive crowds that filled the PT candidate's rallies began to worry his opponents, leading to a decline in the level of the campaign.

Decades later, the lies that would be known as fake news started spreading throughout the state. Rumors circulated that Lula had amassed wealth as a trade unionist and that his house in São Bernardo was merely a façade to deceive people. They claimed he actually lived in an affluent neighborhood in São Paulo.

In response, the party felt compelled to issue a denial. The rumors about Lula's alleged mansion in Morumbi didn't gain traction because he lived in Jardim Lavínia, at Rua Maria Azevedo, 273. Now, they have concocted a fictional holiday home on the beach. However, over the past ten years, the only vacation Lula had was the 31 days he spent in DOPS jail. The party challenged Lula's accusers to come forward and reveal the address of this alleged house in Guarujá and provide its deed.

Despite facing numerous challenges, the PT campaign continued to gain momentum and receive strong support. Even from Paris, the renowned Bahian writer Jorge Amado, who was immensely popular, announced that he would vote for Lula if he lived in São Paulo. Not only did stars from the highly popular Corinthians soccer team declare their support for Lula, but they also organized a mass movement to join the PT.

As election day drew near, two incidents solidified Lula's belief that victory was within reach and that he had already won the election. The first was a debate organized by the newspaper Folha de S.Paulo and

Rede Bandeirantes television, the only one where all candidates participated. Lula, Senator Franco Montoro (PMDB), former President Jânio Quadros (PTB), former mayor of São Paulo Reinaldo de Barros (PDS), and deputy and former basketball player Rogê Ferreira (PDT) all took part. The respected Gallup Institute conducted a poll and the next day all newspapers declared Lula as the clear winner of the debate.

However, what truly solidified Lula's certainty of victory was the rally held in São Paulo's main square, where he attracted a crowd of over 100,000 people according to conservative estimates. The crowd's size even worried Montoro's supporters, who, despite featuring artists like Milton Nascimento and Chico Buarque on stage, failed to attract even half the audience that gathered to hear Lula.

Upon arriving home on the eve of the elections, Lula was greeted by his wife, Marisa. With sadness in her eyes, she showed him an advance edition of "Folha de S.Paulo" that displayed the headline on the front page, spanning eight columns: "Montoro Governor," accompanied by a smiling photo of the PMDB senator and the survey results: "Montoro, 44.8%; Reinaldo, 26.5%; Lula, 12.2%; Jânio, 11.7%; and Rogê Ferreira, 1.7%." Lula burst into laughter, tossing the newspaper in the air, and exclaimed, "This bourgeois newspaper means nothing! I have won the election!"

When the polls opened, the results revealed that Folha's polling data was incorrect. Lula was not in third place, but rather in fourth, behind Montoro, Reinaldo, and Jânio, only surpassing Rogê Ferreira, who received less than 1% of the votes. Lula garnered 1,144,648 votes, which accounted for 10.77% of the total number of voters in the state. The world appeared to crumble around him.

Four decades later, Lula still vividly remembered the profound depression that engulfed him after the defeat. He said, "It hurt. It hurt a lot. I fell into despair, lost my way. I had only one certainty: my political career was over." He experienced a prolonged period of emptiness and humiliation. Adding insult to injury, the union already had another board, leaving him feeling lost and desperate.

8

FROM DEFEAT TO VICTORY

THE SEEMINGLY NEVER-ENDING hangover lasted for over two years. In early 1985, Lula traveled to Cuba, where President Fidel Castro had organized a seminar on the foreign debt of impoverished countries with international financial organizations.

Upon learning of the former union leader's presence in Havana, Fidel requested a private conversation with Lula. Patiently listening to Lula's grievances about the humiliating defeat and frustration, Fidel expressed his desire to retire from politics. In a short but convincing speech, Fidel said, "Listen, Lula: since the invention of voting and elections, no worker... I repeat, no worker, anywhere in the world... has received a million votes like you have. If you allow an older and more experienced person's opinion, hear what I'm saying: you have no right to abandon politics. You have no right to do this to the working class."

Fidel Castro's words echoed in Lula's mind for months. A year later, during the elections for the

National Constituent Assembly, he decided to heed the Commander's advice and run as a candidate. He received an unprecedented 651,763 votes, becoming the most voted federal deputy in Brazil's history up to that point.

In 1986, Lula participated in the Constituent Assembly, despite his discreet role. This did not deter him from running for the Presidency of the Republic for the first time in 1989.

However, Lula ultimately lost the second round to Fernando Collor de Mello. Two years later, the PT (Worker's Party) would take to the streets, demanding Collor's impeachment due to corruption allegations. When Itamar Franco replaced Collor, Lula declined government positions.

In another electoral race, Lula suffered defeat in 1994 at the hands of his old friend Fernando Henrique Cardoso (FHC) from the PSDB (Brazilian Social Democracy Party). FHC, who had served as Itamar's minister and was one of the creators of the Real Plan, was dubbed by Lula as an "electoral embezzler."

This loss came as a shock to the PT candidate, who had even considered forming a moderate ticket with Tasso Jereissatti from the PSDB as his vice-president. However, PT radicals prevented this alliance. Four years later, caught off guard by the constitutional amendment allowing re-election, Lula once again lost to FHC in the first round.

FHC's dwindling popularity during his second term made Lula's victory in 2002 more probable. Alongside political and economic changes, Lula embraced political marketing as a means to centralize his electoral messages.

One pivotal moment was the "Letter to the Brazilian People," in which Lula reassured the market by promising to maintain the macroeconomic foundations established by his predecessor and govern with fiscal responsibility. José Alencar, a businessman, became his confidant and vice president for eight years.

Lula's triumph was secured by defeating José Serra, also from the PSDB. At the titling ceremony at the Superior Electoral Court, Lula shed tears, stating that the diploma for President of the Republic was the first he had ever earned in his life.

Clara Ant, a former advisor who had coordinated Lula's initiatives over the past three decades, described the former president as "a notorious pragmatist." She said, "Lula only broke ties with radicals when they broke ties with him first. This was true of his time as a trade unionist and as a politician. His focus was solely on what could go right."

9

IN POWER

THE LULA GOVERNMENT continued the economic policy of its predecessor, President Fernando Henrique Cardoso. The government's priority remained focused on keeping inflation under control and ensuring the stability of the real.

Lula's administration also capitalized on the favorable external environment, marked by the growth of China and India, as they opened their markets and increased consumption. This led to a surge in the export of raw materials and Brazilian commodities.

Moreover, when the economic crisis hit the United States and Europe in 2008, Brazil managed to weather the storm relatively well. The government implemented measures such as reducing certain taxes, including the Tax on Industrialized Products (IPI), which encompassed household appliances, for instance.

Consequently, the industries refrained from passing on the increased costs to consumers, thereby aiding in maintaining stability within the domestic market. As a result of the crisis and the positive state of the Brazilian economy, foreign businessmen and workers began flocking to Brazil, seeking investment opportunities and livelihoods.

During this period, Brazil also hosted the Pan American Games in 2007, with hopes of securing the bid for the Olympic Games. Subsequently, Brazil successfully obtained the rights to host the World Cup in 2010, the Military Games in 2011, the World Games for Indigenous Peoples in 2015, as well as the Olympics and Paralympics in 2016.

The construction of stadiums and the necessary infrastructure for these events had a significant impact on the local economy and projected an image of prosperity and stability to the international community.

In 2007, the government launched the Growth Acceleration Program (PAC) to enhance the country's infrastructure. President Lula appointed Dilma Rousseff as the program's lead to increase visibility and bolster his candidacy for the 2010 presidential elections.

Over time, the program expanded to address other areas requiring attention, such as childhood, housing, and historic cities. Funding for these programs was intended to come from the federal government and private companies.

Regrettably, contractors seeking to secure contracts and win bids resorted to paying bribes to deputies and senators. In some instances, politicians themselves solicited bribes to expedite projects. This scandal would later emerge as one of the biggest controversies of the Lula government, ultimately unfolding during Dilma's presidency.

During his inauguration speech in 2003, President Lula acknowledged that many Brazilian citizens still struggled to afford three meals a day. Consequently, he called on the nation to unite in the fight against hunger.

As a result, the government implemented various social programs, with the flagship initiative being the "Bolsa-Família" (Family Scholarship) program, where income was directly transferred to eligible families.

To qualify for the program, beneficiaries had to meet specific criteria, such as having a monthly income ranging from 85 to 175 reais and having pregnant women or children aged 0 to 17 within the family. The amount disbursed to families ranged from 35 to 176 reais per month.

In exchange, the family would commit to ensuring that the children attend school regularly and receive regular medical check-ups. This program has been hailed as one of the government's greatest successes, as it has significantly reduced extreme poverty in Brazil by 75% between 2001 and 2014, according to the Food and Agriculture Organization of the United Nations (FAO).

Despite facing criticism from the opposition for being clientelistic, the program has provided many families with access to food, school supplies, and clothing for the first time. The Lula government prioritized education and implemented a plan aimed at democratizing access to schools at all levels across the country. To finance and expand basic education, the government established Fundeb in 2007.

In higher education, the government focused on expanding scholarships for master's and doctoral degrees, with the goal of increasing the number of qualified professors in universities by 5%. The government also expanded access to higher education for the poorest segments of the population through the implementation of social and racial quotas in 20 federal universities across 14 states.

In 2009, the Unified Selection System (Sisu) was created, which selects students for vacancies in federal universities based on their scores in the National High School Examination (Enem). This system allows students from any state in the country to attend a federal university in another state without the need to take another entrance exam.

To further increase the number of available spots, the government opened 14 new federal universities. However, it also allowed private universities to grow by providing public scholarship funding through the Prouni (University for All) program, which was created in 2005.

In terms of foreign policy, the Lula government actively engaged with numerous countries. The president participated in international forums such as Davos and the G-20, where he supported Russia's entry into the group. The government prioritized cooperation with countries like China, India, Russia, and South Africa, leading to the establishment of the BRICS economic alliance.

The government also fostered closer ties with South American countries, particularly through strategic alliances with presidents Néstor Kirchner and Hugo Chávez. These alliances focused on pragmatic objectives such as the construction of refineries and investments in Argentina, rather than purely ideological ones.

Lula also forgave the foreign debt of several African countries, including Nigeria, in order to promote cooperation between developing nations. These measures were part of the government's broader effort to push for reform within the United Nations and secure a permanent seat on the UN Security Council.

While Brazil did not achieve its desired position on the Security Council, it did experience an increase in trade with almost all countries it maintained relations with.

Towards the end of his term, Lula's foreign policy faced controversy when he welcomed the Iranian president, Mahmoud Ahmadinejad, to Brasilia in 2009.

10

RIGHT-WING RESISTANCE

In 2005, a major movement to overthrow Lula's government emerged from the right-wing and big business sectors, with little concern for the country's poorest population. Known as "O mensalão" (The Big Monthly Payment), this was an illicit payment scheme used by the federal government to secure support from deputies and senators for favorable laws and amendments.

The scheme was exposed through hidden camera footage, in which a post office director explained to two businessmen how bids were manipulated. Deputy Roberto Jefferson, an ally of the government, was also implicated in the scheme.

Subsequent investigations led to the establishment of a Parliamentary Commission of Inquiry (CPI), which implicated several allies of the Lula government. Deputy Roberto Jefferson accused the PT treasurer, Delúbio Soares, of making payments to some members of the National Congress. These payments, referred to as "mensalão," were made on a monthly basis.

The revelations resulted in the removal of Minister of the Civil House, José Dirceu, and the disqualification of Deputy Roberto Jefferson for 10 years. Another PT deputy, João da Cunha, was accused of involvement in the plot but resigned before formal accusations could be made against him.

On October 29, 2006, Luís Inácio Lula da Silva from the Workers' Party (PT) was re-elected as the President of the Republic, with José Alencar Gomes da Silva (PRB) as his running mate. In his first speech after his re-election, Lula emphasized that combating poverty would be a top priority in his government, with a focus on the most vulnerable populations. He pledged to govern with equality, prioritizing the needs of all citizens.

In his second term, after achieving fiscal stability, Brazil's fiscal and tax policy shifted towards international competitiveness and the country's development. However, the global crisis of 2007 and 2008 disrupted these plans. At the time of the crisis, Brazil had a strong economy and established institutions, thanks to the continuity of the same macroeconomic foundations implemented since the launch of the Real Plan in 1994.

Starting in 2007, the government implemented expansionary fiscal and monetary policies, including reductions in taxes, interest rates, and demand incentives. Initially, the Brazilian Central Bank acted efficiently and appropriately in response to the external crisis. Measures were promptly taken, supported by the favorable economic, financial, institutional, and political situation that had been built over the previous years. As a result, Brazil withstood the contagion relatively well, being one of the last countries to be affected and one of the first to begin recovering from the external crisis. The surge in commodity prices on the international market, driven by increased imports from China, also aided Brazil during this period.

However, due to the measures taken to combat the external crisis and address internal social inequality, the government neglected public accounts, leading to the emergence of an internal economic crisis that became a legacy for the subsequent administration.

During his four-year term, Lula solidified his social assistance policy, strengthening programs such as Bolsa Família to support the poorest citizens. Lula successfully controlled inflation and reduced the unemployment rate in the country. In 2010, the final year of Lula's presidency, the unemployment rate stood at 6.7%, according to the Brazilian Institute of Geography and Statistics (IBGE). In comparison, the unemployment rate in the first quarter of 2022 was 11.1%.

Under Lula's government, Brazil implemented the Growth Acceleration Program (PAC), which included infrastructure projects such as the construction of ports, highways, railroads, and investments in basic sanitation. With these improvements, Brazil became a member of the BRICS, an economic bloc comprising Russia, India, China, and South Africa. Brazil also joined the G-20, a group of the world's 20 largest economies. During a meeting of G-20 leaders in London in 2009, then-US

President Barack Obama greeted Lula, saying, "This is the guy. I love this guy."

Education was another focus of the PT government under Lula's leadership. He established the University for All Program (Prouni), which provided scholarships to economically disadvantaged students to study at private universities across the country.

During Lula's presidency, more than 20 million Brazilians lifted themselves out of poverty and entered the middle class (C class) with family incomes between R$1,126 and R$4,854. A study by the Getúlio Vargas Foundation found that poverty in Brazil decreased by 50.6% under Lula's government.

Lula concluded his second term in 2010 with an 87% approval rating. He successfully supported Dilma Rousseff's election as his successor, and she assumed office in 2011.

Dilma Rousseff's story would certainly warrant another biography, but it is worth noting that during her second term as president, she was impeached as part of a major political scheme that ultimately removed her from office for something that became legal the following year. This impeachment was orchestrated by center-right politicians who believed they would soon seize power. It was carried out under the leadership of Dilma's vice president, Michel Temer, who assumed the presidency after the impeachment. However, these neoliberals did not anticipate the rise of the Brazilian extreme right, which gained support from violent and criminal elements in the country, as well as neo-Pentecostal churches. This shift led to the election of Jair

Bolsonaro, a fascist and neo-Nazi figure, who committed numerous crimes while in power under the umbrella of fascism and with the support of corrupt and money laundering neo-Pentecostal churches.

Meanwhile, Lula continued with his life, delivering lectures worldwide and taking rest whenever possible.

However, in 2018, the country witnessed the implementation of the largest criminal scheme in its history to prevent Lula from running in the 2018 elections and to ensure the victory of the extreme right, which had already gained control over various sectors of society.

11

HIGH NOON

On the afternoon of Thursday, April 5, 2018, employees at the Lula Institute closed drawers and turned off computers. In a small meeting room, former President Dilma Rousseff, Senator Cid Gomes from the Brazilian state of Ceará's PDT, and Senator Gleisi Hoffmann, president of the Workers' Party, gathered behind closed doors, drinking coffee and engaging in conversation.

Lula's lawyers, Valeska Teixeira and Cristiano Zanin, bid farewell to the remaining individuals and left. Just minutes earlier, they had announced that an arrest warrant had been issued for Lula.

Inside the institute, there was no tension, but rather a mood of somber anticipation. The Supreme Court's decision that morning, denying the ex-president's defense yet another request for habeas corpus, had opened the doors for the worst-case scenario: the arrest of Lula by Judge Sergio Moro. From a strictly legal standpoint, everyone at the institute knew that arrest could be decreed at any moment after the Supreme Court's decision. However, the general feeling was that immediate arrest was unjustified. It was expected that Moro would issue the warrant at the beginning of the following week.

Not everyone shared this expectation. Some of Lula's associates believed that the arrest was imminent and could happen before the end of the day. Lula himself, however, was confident that he would spend the weekend in freedom. He left his office on the second floor and went down the spiral stairs to a small hall, where he asked his young advisor Marco Aurélio Santana Ribeiro to put him in contact with Moisés Selerges. Lula requested Moisés to organize a "half secret" barbecue for a small group of friends on Saturday morning at the union. It would be an opportunity for Lula to relax and enjoy some barbecue ribs and cachacinha.

As Marcola waited for the call to end and return her cell phone, she was surprised to see the lawyers Valeska and Zanin return through the door, visibly upset. Valeska showed Marcola her cell phone screen with the headline that would soon spread across the planet: "Moro decrees Lula's arrest." The couple of lawyers, accustomed to the notoriously slow pace of justice, had not anticipated that the judges of the Federal Regional Court could act so quickly. That same afternoon, the process was released for Moro to decree the prison.

In the final three paragraphs of the sentence published on the internet, the magistrate transformed the defendant's rights into "concessions" based on his position as a former president. Lula was granted the opportunity to voluntarily present himself to the

Federal Police in Curitiba by 5:00 pm on 04/06/2018, when the arrest warrant would be served. The use of handcuffs was prohibited, and a reserved room was prepared for the former president's sentence to ensure his moral and physical integrity.

With the declaration of Lula's arrest, Moro solidified his position as the leader of a political earthquake that had begun four years earlier with the Lava Jato Operation. Through an impressive propaganda machine, Moro had been portrayed as a superhero and national hero, a provincial judge from Paraná who led an unprecedented war on corruption. He sentenced almost a hundred politicians, businessmen, and ordinary citizens, catching them in the operation's crossfire.

However, not everyone succumbed to this violence. This resistance was not limited to PT militants like João Vaccari Neto, who spent two years in prison without opening his mouth, despite his family members being persecuted. The fight against corruption continued, with some refusing to be silenced.

According to the Brazilian Justice's quiet bureaucracy, the decisions leading up to Lula's arrest were made astonishingly fast, raising suspicions of prearrangement among the three judicial instances. Thanks to the precise electronic recording of votes and documents, it is known that the Supreme Court denied Lula's habeas corpus by a vote of 6 to 5 at 12:48 a.m. The decision was then transmitted to the court's computers in Porto Alegre at dawn.

On the same day, at precisely 5:32:20 p.m., the court sent the authorization for arrest to the 13th

Federal Court in Curitiba. At 5:50:10 p.m., Judge Sergio Moro, the head of the court, decreed Lula's arrest.

From the moment the document arrived in Curitiba, Moro defied the prevailing norm in Brazil, where court cases often languish for months or even years, by taking just seventeen minutes to execute Lula's arrest.

Still grappling with how to respond to the news from Curitiba, the city of Lava-Jato and the entire plot, Lula absentmindedly tugged at his mustache, a familiar habit, as he listened to the opinions of those around him. Moraes approached him and said, "Mr. President, the streets are unsafe. We need to leave before any provocation or incident occurs."

Outside the institute, the atmosphere felt like a prelude to what would unfold in the next 48 hours. Alongside half a dozen journalists stationed on the sidewalk, a crowd gathered on the narrow, steep street. Onlookers, newspaper reporters, blog networks, and radio and television broadcasters were all present, eagerly awaiting developments.

Moto couriers weaved through the crowd, carrying cameramen on their backs, all hoping to capture a glimpse of the former president. Cameramen and photographers positioned themselves on the ground, on motorcycles, on van rooftops, and even in helicopters belonging to major broadcasting companies, all with their lenses trained on the underground garage entrance of the institute, through which Lula was expected to exit.

News of the events spread rapidly across the internet, radio, and television, attracting both supporters and opponents of Lula's imprisonment. The institute's front was soon swarmed by people, blocking traffic and creating a cacophony of honking horns that disrupted the peace of the neighboring residents.

As Lula's convoy departed, it avoided the main garage where the mob awaited, opting instead for an alternate route. However, the incident feared by Captain Moraes ultimately occurred. When Senator Lindbergh Farias, state deputy Emidio de Souza (PT), and former federal deputy Márcio Macedo (PT) were identified at the institute's entrance, a small business owner named Carlos Alberto Bettoni, 56, emerged from a group of anti-Lula protesters. Bettoni advanced toward the three politicians, pointing a finger at them and shouting, "Lula thief! Thief Lula!" PT activists surrounded Bettoni, and someone punched him in the face. Losing his balance, Bettoni struck his head on the bumper of a stationary truck in the traffic jam, falling unconscious with blood streaming from his forehead. He later regained consciousness, stood up, and was taken, staggering, to a nearby hospital, where it was determined that he had sustained a minor head injury.

The aggressors received twelve days of preventive detention and faced charges of attempted murder.

As Lula's car made its way from the institute to the union, a distance of twenty kilometers, it was met with shouts of "Thief! Thief!" as well as fireworks and attacks on vehicles by anti-Lula groups.

The news and the presence of media vehicles and moto couriers attracted even more people. To evade persecution and provocation, Moraes ordered the driver to change the route. Despite the high speed, the car carrying Lula continued to be pursued by increasingly enraged Brazilians, manipulated and alienated by the media. Some of the more aggressive protesters went beyond verbal insults, striking Brazilian flagpoles on the roofs of cars and hurling profanities.

In the first two vehicles, six of the ex-president's armed security guards experienced an unprecedented test of nerves. Despite the chaos surrounding them, Lula appeared calm, engaging in conversations and making and receiving phone calls, seemingly unaffected by the savagery that had taken hold of the streets. Night had fallen, and there was no indication that the situation would improve.

The union block, where Lula would reside until he made a decision about his next steps, was occupied by his supporters. To reach the building's entrance by car, Lula had to navigate a human chain slowly. Hundreds of workers, union leaders, activists, intellectuals, artists, and politicians from various states cleared a path for Lula and blocked all entrances and exits of the building. Only two members of Lula's security detail, Lieutenant Rogério dos Santos and Sergeant Elias dos Reis, remained with him.

The crowd shouted in unison, "Don't surrender! Don't surrender! Don't surrender!"

At a safe distance of two hundred meters, but clearly visible to the demonstrators, a platoon of agents from the Federal Police's Tactical Operations Command stood.

Compared to the crowd surrounding the building, there weren't many, perhaps a few dozen. However, they appeared menacing and prepared for combat. They were heavily armed and equipped, as if they were going to war. They awaited any order to arrest Lula.

Philosopher and political activist Guilherme Boulos, leader of the Homeless Workers Movement and the Socialism and Freedom Party, received news of the arrest warrant. He had just returned from a political tour of the Northeast, where he had discussed his pre-candidacy for the President of the Republic in the October elections. Boulos decided to go to the Lula Institute, but on the way, he received a call from Marcola informing him that the former president had already left for the union, where Boulos was also supposed to go.

Boulos's destination was the ABC region when he arrived in São Paulo. He was already late for an assembly called by the "Povo sem Medo occupation" (People Without Fear occupation), a mega-camp of 60 thousand square meters in front of the Scania factory in São Bernardo, São Paulo. Eight thousand displaced families had been living there for six months under nylon tents.

The Thursday assembly aimed to celebrate and organize the successful demobilization of those encamped, who were leaving the place. In exchange for vacating the land, owned by a construction company, the governor of the state, Geraldo Alckmin, had signed a protocol with Boulos, committing to build and deliver 2400 housing units for the homeless in the camp.

On his way, Boulos called Josué Rocha from the direction of the landless movement and Andreia Barbosa, coordinator of the occupation. He suggested that they put up for discussion, in the ongoing assembly, the proposal for everyone to move to the union, one kilometer from the camp. "This prison is arbitrary, absurd, a political prison!" Boulos shouted into the phone. "Everyone has to go to São Bernardo and ensure democratic resistance. We will not passively accept this nonsense!"

After being put to a vote, the proposal was unanimously approved. Minutes later, a mass of people caused further chaos in the traffic on the Anchieta highway, as they made their way to the union, which had turned into a bunker for the former president.

Only the elderly and those with mobility difficulties remained in the occupation. When Boulos finally reached the union, around 5,000 people were already there, including activists, workers, and militants. They waved red flags and chanted slogans: "Don't surrender! Don't surrender! Surround and don't get caught! 'Lula doesn't come out!' Federal does not enter!"

Informed of Moro's decision, the PT's Central Única dos Trabalhadores (CUT) posted a note on social networks, urging its affiliates to join the vigil in front of the union. "We must continue to resist, defending the greatest political leader this country has ever had," the note said. "To defend Lula is to defend democracy."

Adding to the metallurgists and militants who took to the streets around the building, it was estimated that there were around 10,000 people willing to camp there until Lula decided what to do next.

Despite the strict security barriers at the entrance doors, the inside of the union was overflowing. Even during the height of the ABC strikes in the 1970s and 1980s, such a massive crowd had never been seen before. Politicians, activists, and militants from all over the country flocked there and mingled with intellectuals, TV and film artists, nuns, rappers, and numerous journalists and photographers.

Only the news website Jornalistas Livres (Free Journalists), self-titled "A collective without a boss, editor, marketer, or censor," managed to have eighteen young people inside the building, filming everything with their cell phones. Each scene captured was immediately posted on the internet and broadcasted.

Attracted by the news, street vendors suddenly appeared, selling "Lula Livre" (Free Lula) flags, t-shirts, caps, and pushing carts with mineral water, coconut water, beer - a true informal trade.

On the second floor, where Lula had been taken, the only decision made unanimously was that he would sleep in the union. They placed a double mattress in a room with difficult access, in the basement of the building, the last in a labyrinth of gray corridors, squeezed between dividing walls and a platform. Allies also went to the ex-president's apartment, gathered two sets of clothes, and put them in a small suitcase.

Regarding the most serious and important decision - how to react to the arrest order - the political group closest to Lula was divided. Senators Lindbergh Farias, Gleisi Hoffmann, lawyer Luiz Eduardo Greenhalgh, who had accompanied Lula for thirty years, and activists João Pedro Stédile and

Guilherme Boulos, among others, argued that Moro's sentence should simply be ignored, thus transferring the problem to the opponents. For them, the watchword was "resist."

The security forces, in their imagination, would never commit the insanity of massacring the crowd surrounding the union to arrest Lula. This impasse, once it became global news, was seen by the resistance supporters as an opportunity to expose the persecution of Lula by Moro, the Public Ministry, and the Federal Police to the world. Despite the surprising proposal from two party leaders and the leaders of the landless, who were the most relevant social movements in the country, lawyers Valeska and Zanin heard it with surprise. Although they vigorously defended Lula as a victim of "lawfare" both in Brazil and abroad, they knew that failing to comply with the arrest warrant would inevitably lead Moro to consider Lula a fugitive and issue a preventive detention order, making it nearly impossible to obtain a habeas corpus for the former president.

The essential question of whether to surrender or resist remained unanswered. Captain Valmir Moraes, an experienced officer, listened silently with concern, refraining from expressing his opinion to anyone. He knew that the Federal Police lacked the structure and training to disperse crowds, and he feared that a confrontation would quickly escalate into a massacre, as a single rifle shot could be enough to claim the lives of several people.

Unbeknownst to many, the São Paulo Military Police were also on high alert. Concealed within a small forest less than a kilometer away from the union, riot squad troops waited inside four gray buses and two armored vehicles known as "caveirões" (Big skulls). Prepared for war, the soldiers were accompanied by a pack of intimidating Rottweilers and German shepherds and armed with rubber bullets and tear gas launchers.

All it would take was an order from the command in São Paulo for the soldiers to disperse the stubborn mass gathered at the union's entrance and forcefully pave the way for the federal agents to enter the building and arrest Lula.

As the night wore on, the union and the surrounding streets became even more crowded. The 24-hour deadline imposed by Moro was rapidly approaching, and no one present knew how the situation would be resolved. Would Lula give in or resist? Lula had no desire to surrender. After all, why would an innocent person want to?

Before the arrest, Lula's lawyers presented yet another argument to refute the accusations against their client: Lula was a victim of "lawfare."

But what exactly is "lawfare"? In simple terms, it is a form of warfare conducted through the manipulation of laws to target individuals who have been elected as political enemies. It involves the often abusive use of the law as a weapon in war. It is a strategy that utilizes, or rather exploits, the law as a substitute for traditional military methods to achieve success in conflicts.

In a democracy, it is crucial that the law be followed. Therefore, the state utilizes the law to target those it considers as enemies. This approach gives an appearance of legality to abuses. It's similar to when someone claims that even though impeachment followed legal procedures, it was still considered a coup. It's like the devil using the words of God to tempt Jesus. Those who defend this viewpoint argue that there was a phenomenon known as Lawfare in Brazil, and that Dilma was defeated as a result.

According to Lula's lawyers, the practice of Lawfare involves manipulating the legal system, abusing rights, attempting to influence public opinion, politicizing the judicial process, and causing disillusionment among the people. The concept of "legal war" implies that a political group will use the law to hinder or punish the actions of another political group. Lula's defense argues that the Ministry of Public Affairs' involvement is not only legal but also political.

Lula's lawyers claim that his opponents resort to Lawfare because they cannot defeat him in the polls. Lawfare, in this context, refers to a political tactic aimed at ousting him from power. Undoubtedly, using Lawfare is more efficient and less exhausting than winning an election. There is nothing more effective than legally dismantling an opponent, even if it is disguised.

Lawfare is inherently negative; it is the opposite of seeking justice. It involves filing frivolous lawsuits and misusing legal processes to intimidate and frustrate adversaries. In a Lawfare, the side with the most power wins, whether it be political or economic. This form of warfare is not new on the international stage.

This tactical excuse has now arrived in Brazil. On April 7, 2018, amidst a media spectacle, Lula was arrested. Prior to his arrest, he delivered a historic speech to thousands of hopeful individuals seeking justice in Brazil.

However, their hopes were in vain. Lula was transported to Curitiba, a conservative capital and the birthplace of Operation Lava-Jato, where he would spend the next 580 days as a political prisoner.

His arrest followed a conviction in the second instance for corruption and money laundering in the Guarujá triplex case. According to the Lava Jato operation, the property was allegedly given to Lula as a bribe payment from OAS, a construction company, in exchange for contracts with Petrobras. Lula denies these allegations.

For 82 weeks, Lula, despite being imprisoned, remained politically active, engaging in party politics, actively participating in Fernando Haddad's presidential campaign, giving interviews, providing testimonies, and even revealing a romance.

Since April 7, 2018, the former president resided in a small 15-square-meter bedroom with a bathroom. This space, originally intended for police officers visiting Paraná, was adapted to resemble a larger state room as a gesture of respect for Lula's previous position as head of state.

Dramatic moments were not in short supply. While in prison, Lula learned of the death of his grandson Arthur, who succumbed to a bacterial infection. Judge Carolina Lebbos, responsible for executing his sentence, granted him permission to leave prison and attend the funeral in São Bernardo do Campo (SP).

Prior to this, Lula experienced two other losses while behind bars. He was not allowed to bid farewell to his older brother, Genival Inácio da Silva, also known as Vavá, who was suffering from cancer. Additionally, he was unable to say goodbye to his friend Sigmaringa Seixas, a lawyer and former PT deputy.

Rumors spread among PT members that this series of misfortunes had left Lula in a state of depression. However, those who accompanied him insisted that he remained strong. Lawyer Luiz Carlos da Rocha, also known as Rochinha, who visited the president during that time, stated that Lula was angry but not depressed.

Fifteen days after his arrest, Lula received a book by Arun Gandhi, grandson of the Indian pacifist Mahatma Gandhi. The book explores Ghandi's teachings on channeling anger into non-violent actions. Lula read the book, but his anger persisted. He directed his anger towards Sergio Moro, the current Minister of Justice under President Jair Bolsonaro. Moro had previously sentenced Lula in the first instance of the triplex case during his tenure as the judge responsible for the Lava Jato operation.

Throughout his time in prison, the former president repeatedly claimed to be a victim of persecution by Moro, accusing him of playing politics with his case. Lula regarded Moro's appointment as Minister of Justice by President Bolsonaro as evidence of the judge's electoral agenda.

With the subsequent revelations of exchanged messages between Moro and Lava Jato prosecutors, Lula began to assert that there was no longer any doubt about the partiality of the magistrate, who was acting as both judge and accuser.

Obtained by The Intercept Brasil and published on their website as well as other media outlets, such as Folha, the messages raised doubts about the behavior of the former judge and members of the task force. This ultimately resulted in the weakening of the Lava Jato operation.

In the prison cell where Lula resided, there were amenities such as a TV, radio, and an ergometric treadmill. The former president utilized the treadmill for walks and exercise, using elastic bands to engage the muscles in his arms and legs.

Television served as Lula's primary pastime. Through news programs, he watched series and films provided by his lawyers on a pendrive. He even took an interest in religious programs, recognizing the political influence of priests and pastors, which he believed had grown more significant in the current state of the country.

However, the decision to isolate Lula in a separate cell away from other prisoners resulted in a significant degree of solitude. He spent approximately 22 hours per day alone, with only one-hour visits from his lawyers in the morning and afternoon. On weekends, he had no contact with anyone except for the jailers.

During his time in prison Lula penned a manifest to the people of Brazil. This remarkable document is worth including in its entirety. You can read it in the following chapter.

12

MANIFEST TO THE PEOPLE OF BRAZIL

"*For two months now, I have been unjustly incarcerated without having committed any crime. For two months I have been unable to travel the country I love, bringing the message of hope of a better and more just Brazil, with opportunities for all, as I always did during 45 years of public life.*

I was deprived of my daily life with my sons and my daughter, my grandsons and granddaughters, my great-granddaughter, my friends and comrades. But I have no doubt that they have put me here to prevent me from being with my larger family: the Brazilian people. This is what distresses me the most, because I know that outside, every day, more and more families are back to living in the streets, abandoned by the State that should protect them.

From where I am, I want to renew the message of faith in Brazil and in our people. Together, we have been able to overcome difficult times, serious economic, political and social crises. Together, under my government, we overcame hunger, unemployment, recession, the enormous pressures of international capital and its representatives in the country. Together, we reduced the age-old disease of social inequality that marked Brazil's formation: indigenous genocide, the enslavement of blacks and the exploitation of the workers of the city and the countryside.

We fought injustice tirelessly. With our heads held high, we have come to be considered the most optimistic people in the world. We have deepened our democracy and we have gained international prominence with the creation of UNASUR, CELAC, BRICS and our relationship of solidarity with African countries. Our voice was heard in the G8 and in the most important world fora.

I am sure we can rebuild this country and dream, once again, like a great nation. That's what keeps me fighting.

I will not settle with the suffering of the poorest and the punishment that is falling on our working class, just as I will not settle with my situation.

Those who accused me in Lava Jato know that they lied, because I never owned, never had possession, nor spent one night in the Guarujá apartment. Those who condemned me, Sérgio Moro and the TRF-4 judges, know that they set up a judicial farce to arrest me because I was able to prove my innocence in the case and they were not able to present proof of the crime that they accuse me of.

To this day I ask myself: where is the proof?

I was not treated by the prosecutors of Lava Jato, Moro and TRF-4 as a citizen equal to everyone else. I have always been treated as an enemy.

I do not cultivate hatred or hold any grudge, but I doubt my executioners can sleep with a clear conscience.

Against all injustices, I have the constitutional right to appeal out of jail, but this right has been denied to me so far, for the sole reason that my name is Luiz Inácio Lula da Silva.

That is why I consider myself a political prisoner in my country.

When it became clear that they were going to take me in by force, without crime or evidence, I decided to stay in Brazil and face my executioners. I know my place in history and I know the place reserved for those who persecute me today. I am sure that Justice will make truth prevail.

In the caravans I recently took part in, along Brazil, I saw hope in people's eyes. And I have also seen the anguish of those who are suffering with the return of hunger and unemployment, malnourishment, school dropout, rights robbed from workers, destruction of the constitutionally guaranteed policies of social inclusion, that are now denied in practice.

It is to end the suffering of the people that I am again running for President.

I take on this mission because I have a great responsibility with Brazil and because Brazilians have the right to vote freely for a project of more solidarity, a more just and a sovereign country, persevering in the project of Latin American integration.

I am a candidate because I sincerely believe that the Electoral Court will be coherent with its judicial precedents, since 2002, not bowing to the blackmail of exception only to hurt my right and the right of voters to choose who represents them best.

I ran many times during my career, but this race is different: it is my life's commitment. Those who had the privilege of seeing Brazil advance on behalf of the poorest, after centuries of exclusion and abandonment, cannot sit out during the most difficult time for our people.

I know that my candidacy represents hope, and we will take it to the final consequences, because we have the strength of the people at our side.

We have the right to dream again, after the nightmare that was imposed on us by the 2016 coup.

They lied to overthrow the legitimately elected President Dilma Rousseff. They lied saying that the country would improve if the Workers' Party was ousted from government; that there would be more jobs and more development. They lied to impose the program that was defeated at the polls in 2014. They lied to destroy the project of eradicating misery which we put in place under my government. They lied to give away the nation's wealth and to favor the economic and financial powers, in a scandalous betrayal of the people's will manifested clearly and unequivocally in 2002, 2006, 2010 and 2014.

The hour of truth is coming.

I want to be president of Brazil once again because I have already proved that it is possible to build a better Brazil for our people. We proved that the country can grow for the benefit of all when the government places the workers and the poorest at the center of the concerns, and does not become a slave to the interests of the rich and powerful. And we proved that only the inclusion of millions of poor people can make the economy grow and recover.

We govern for the people and not for the market. It is

the opposite of what the government of our opponents, at the service of financiers and multinationals, who abolished the historic rights of workers, reduced real wages, cut off investments in health and education, and is destroying programs like Bolsa Familia, Minha Casa, Minha Vida, Pronaf, Luz Para Todos, Prouni and Fies, among many actions aimed at social justice.

I dream of being president of Brazil to end the suffering of those who do not have money anymore to buy gas, who now have to use wood for cooking or, even worse, use alcohol and become victims of serious accidents and burns. This is one of the cruelest setbacks caused by the policy of destruction of Petrobras and of our national sovereignty, led by PSDB supporters who backed the 2016 coup.

Petrobras was not created to generate gains for Wall Street speculators in New York, but to ensure oil self-sufficiency in Brazil at prices compatible with the popular economy. Petrobras must be Brazilian again. You can be certain that we are going to end this tale of selling its assets. It will no longer be hostage to oil multinationals. It will once again play a strategic role in the country's development, including in directing the pre-salt resources to education, our passport to the future.

You can also be sure that we will prevent the privatization of Eletrobrás, Banco do Brasil and Caixa, the emptying of the BNDES and of all the tools available to the country to promote development and social welfare.

I dream of being the president of a country where the judge pays more attention to the Constitution and less to the headlines.

Where rule of law is the rule, without measures of exception.

I dream of a country where democracy prevails over anyone's discretion, media monopoly, prejudice and discrimination.

I dream of being the president of a country where everyone has rights and nobody has privileges. A country where everyone can have three meals a day again; where children can attend school, where everyone has the right to work for dignified wages and with the protection of the law. A country in which every rural worker has again access to land to produce, with finance and technical assistance.

A country where people will once again have confidence in the present and hope for the future. And where for this very reason is once again respected internationally, promotes Latin American integration and cooperation with Africa once again, and exercises a sovereign position in the international dialogues on trade and the environment, for peace and friendship amongst peoples.

We know the way to carry out these dreams. Today it goes through the holding of free and democratic elections, with the participation of all political forces, with no rules of exception to prevent just one candidate.

Only then will we have a government with legitimacy to face great challenges, that can dialogue with all sectors of the nation supported by the popular vote. It is this mission that I am taking on by accepting my nomination as presidential candidate of the Workers' Party.

We have demonstrated already that it is possible to make a government of national appeasement, where which Brazil walks in the direction of the Brazilians, especially the poorest and the workers.

My government was one where the poor were

included in the Union's budget, with more income distribution and less hunger; with more health and less child mortality; with more respect and affirmation of the rights of women, of blacks and of diversity, and with less violence; with more education at all levels and fewer children out of school; with more access to universities and technical education and fewer young people excluded from the future; with more popular housing and fewer occupancy conflicts in the cities; with more settlements and land distribution and fewer conflicts of occupation in the countryside; with more respect for the indigenous populations and quilombolas, with more salary gains and guarantees for the rights of workers, with more dialogue with unions, social movements and business organizations and less social conflicts.

It was a time of peace and prosperity, as we have never had before in history.

I believe, from the bottom of my heart, that Brazil can be happy again. And it can advance much more than we had already conquered together, when the government was of the people.

In order to achieve this goal, we must unite the democratic forces of all Brazil, respecting the autonomy of the parties and the movements, but always having as reference a project of more solidarity and a fairer Country that will rescue the dignity and hope of our suffering people. I am sure we will be together at the end of that path.

From where I am, with the solidarity and energies that come from all corners of Brazil and the world, I can assure you that I will continue working to transform our dreams into reality. And so I am preparing, with faith in

God and a lot of confidence, for the day when I will once again unite with the beloved Brazilian people.

Only, if my life is taken, will this reunion not come to be.

And this reunion will not happen only if my life is lacking.

See you soon, my people.

Long live Brazil! Long live Democracy! Long live the Brazilian people!"

1 3

───────────

FREEDOM

THE FEDERAL AGENT Jorge Chastalo Filho, who served as the head of the Federal Police agents in Paraná, became the person with whom Lula had the most interaction during his imprisonment. Chastalo was responsible for unlocking Lula's cell at 8 am and locking it at 5 pm.

When Lula first arrived at the prison, Chastalo was the one who escorted him to his cell. On Friday, November 8, 2019, it was Chastalo who delivered the news of Lula's impending release. "Permit signed," the agent announced, to which Lula responded with a smile. Chastalo then accompanied Lula down the four floors of the fire escape to the building's exit.

After facing numerous legal setbacks, including political and persecutory decisions that expedited his cases and denied several appeals seeking to prove his innocence, former president Luiz Inácio Lula da Silva finally left prison on the afternoon of November 8, after enduring 580 days of politically motivated incarceration.

Lula expressed his gratitude to the Brazilian people, referring to them as the nourishment of democracy that sustained him in the face of the malice and villainy demonstrated by certain sectors of the Brazilian state, including the judiciary, the Public Ministry, the Federal Police, and the Federal Revenue. These entities worked towards criminalizing the PT (Workers' Party) and Lula himself. Lula emphasized that his imprisonment was not merely an attempt to detain a man but to extinguish an idea. According to him, ideas cannot be killed or erased.

During his speech, Lula criticized the government of Jair Bolsonaro and highlighted the precarious conditions faced by Brazilian workers. He lamented the fact that people are forced to work as Uber drivers or deliver pizzas by bicycle without receiving due respect.

The former president also condemned the Lava Jato operation, considering it a legal farce designed to convict and imprison him. Lula boldly asserted that even if one were to combine Judge Sérgio Moro and prosecutor Deltan Dallagnol, their combined honesty would not even amount to 10% of his own.

Lula is set to travel to São Bernardo do Campo and deliver an address to the nation at around 10 am on Saturday at the São Bernardo Metallurgical Union. This location holds significance as it is where Lula departed on April 7, 2018, to surrender himself to the Federal Police in compliance with Sérgio Moro's conviction.

Similar to his arrest in April 2018, a crowd eagerly awaited Lula's release outside the Federal Police headquarters in Curitiba, shouting chants and expressing their support. Upon leaving the cell, Lula addressed the dedicated supporters who had been present throughout his imprisonment, expressing his gratitude for their unwavering support. Following this, he proceeded to São Bernardo do Campo, where he will deliver his speech on Saturday morning, the 9th.

Lula's release came one day after the Federal Supreme Court's decision, with a 6 to 5 majority, against the anticipation of sentencing for defendants convicted in the second instance.

The following are the key moments from Lula's speech:

• Lula expressed his heartfelt appreciation for being able to address the crowd.

• He expressed his astonishment at having the opportunity to communicate with the men and women who, for 580 days, greeted him with "good morning, Lula," "good afternoon, Lula," and "good night, Lula," regardless of the weather conditions.

• Lula acknowledged that the steadfast support of the people was the nourishment of democracy that allowed him to resist the injustices perpetrated by a corrupt faction within the justice system against both himself and the Brazilian people.

• He couldn't leave without acknowledging and greeting the supporters who had been present throughout his imprisonment.

• Lula also extended his greetings to Fernando Haddad, the PT's candidate for president, emphasizing that Haddad was almost elected if not for the theft of the election.

• Lula admitted that he had not initially planned to mention the vigil attendees during his speech, but their songs and presence had meant a great deal to him during his time in confinement. He expressed his desire to personally greet and embrace each of them, emphasizing their importance in his life.

• Lula asserted that the unscrupulous side of the Federal Police, the MPF task force, and Moro needed to understand that they did not imprison a man; they attempted to extinguish an idea. He proclaimed that no matter their efforts, ideas cannot be killed or erased. Furthermore, he vowed to fight against the deception orchestrated by these entities, led by Globo, the largest media network in Brazil, which sought to criminalize the PT.

On November 8, 2019, the PT man descended the fire stairs at the rear of the Federal Police building, employing a tactic to mislead the press. He did not carry anything in his hands. The items left behind will be entrusted to an aide during the week.

Lula did not pack his belongings. The photographs of his family and his girlfriend remained on the wall, while his clothes lay in the corners. Everything remained as it had been during the 580 days that the former president resided in a room transformed into a cell on the fourth floor of the Superintendence of the Federal Police in Curitiba. A gathering of lawyers and PT supporters assembled in his cell, and a police officer relayed the news of his freedom to him.

Below is a condensed timeline of the key events that led to Lula's imprisonment and the subsequent annulment of his convictions:

• March 4, 2016: Sérgio Moro orders the Federal

Police to conduct a coercive conduct on former President Luiz Inácio Lula da Silva.

• July 29, 2016: Lula faces criminal charges for obstruction of justice, but is acquitted.

• September 20, 2016: Lula becomes a defendant for passive corruption and money laundering, accused of receiving bribes in the form of property improvements.

• December 19, 2016: Lula faces additional charges of corruption and money laundering related to the purchase of apartments.

• May 10, 2017: Lula denies ownership of a triplex during his testimony to Judge Sérgio Moro.

• July 12, 2017: Lula is sentenced to nine years and six months in prison for corruption and money laundering in the Triplex case.

• August 1, 2017: Lula faces a third accusation of corruption and money laundering related to a property in Atibaia.

• January 24, 2018: Lula's prison sentence is extended to 12 years and one month.

• April 5, 2018: Sérgio Moro issues an arrest warrant for Lula.

• April 7, 2018: Lula is taken into custody and begins serving his sentence in Curitiba.

• May 10, 2018: The Federal Supreme Court denies Lula's request for freedom.

• February 6, 2019: Lula is sentenced to 12 years and 11 months in another corruption case.

• February 21, 2019: Lula's request for freedom is denied by the Federal Supreme Court.

• June 9, 2019: "The Intercept" publishes leaked

conversations exposing Sergio Moro's conduct during Lava Jato investigations.

• November 8, 2019: Lula is released after the Supreme Federal Court deems his arrest unconstitutional.

• January 24, 2021: Lula's defense gains access to seized messages from Operation Spoofing.

• February 1, 2021: The proceedings related to Operation Spoofing are made public.

• March 8, 2021: Lula's convictions are annulled by STF Minister Edson Fachin, making him eligible to run in the 2022 elections.

• March 9, 2021: Gilmar Mendes guides the analysis of Sérgio Moro's suspicion during a session of the Second Panel.

14

A NEW CAMPAIGN

DURING HIS 580-DAY DETENTION, ordered by then-judge Sergio Moro, Lula not only lost his freedom of movement but also the opportunity to run for and defeat Jair Bolsonaro (PL) in the race for the Presidential building, known as the Planalto Palace, that year.

The 12-year prison sentence significantly impacted the 2018 elections, which were characterized by anti-PT sentiment following the corruption scandals linked to Operation Lava Jato. At that time, Lula was leading in the polls.

In the second week of September, the PT officially announced that Fernando Haddad, the former mayor of São Paulo, would replace Lula on the ballot. Subsequently, major institutes began to indicate Bolsonaro as the favorite.

In the first round, Bolsonaro received 49.3 million votes, accounting for 46% of the valid votes, securing the lead and advancing to the second round against Haddad, who received 31.3 million votes (29%).

In the second round, Bolsonaro was elected president of Brazil with the support of 57.8 million voters, equivalent to 55% of the valid votes.

Conveniently in 2019, Sergio Moro left his judicial career to assume the position of Minister of Justice and Public Security, recommended by Bolsonaro.

The appointment of the former judge to oversee the portfolio, which includes the Federal Police, sparked criticism as it strongly suggested that Moro had acted politically by arresting Lula and removing him from the electoral race.

On November 8, 2019, Lula was released from the Federal Police Superintendence in Curitiba after spending 580 days in prison. He stated, "I leave here without hate. At the age of 74, my heart only has room for love because it is love that will prevail in this country."

Lula benefited from a decision by the STF, which ruled that arrests could only occur after a final decision, not after a conviction in the second instance, reversing the court's previous stance in 2016.

Moro's tenure in the Bolsonaro government did not last long, just like Lula's imprisonment. He left office in April 2021 and accused the president of attempting to politically interfere with the Federal Police. This accusation led to an ongoing investigation in the Federal Supreme Court.

In March, the court's plenary determined that Moro had acted in a biased manner in cases involving Lula. The matter was ultimately decided by the 2nd Panel of the STF in favor of Moro's suspicion by a vote of 3 to 2.

By March 2022, all lawsuits involving Lula had either been dismissed or archived due to lack of evidence or statute of limitations.

On May 7, 2022, Lula officially launched his candidacy for President of the Republic. He was the first to announce his vice-presidential candidate: Geraldo Alckmin, the former governor of São Paulo from the PSB party. The alliance between former political adversaries, united against Bolsonaro, was an unprecedented development.

Alckmin declared that no past disagreements or potential future disputes would hinder his unwavering support for Lula's return to the presidency, emphasizing the need for a peaceful, centered, and responsible government.

With Alckmin as his running mate, Lula demonstrated a commitment to a collaborative government, helping to alleviate concerns about his candidacy. Alckmin's presence greatly contributed to the market's confidence in the PT candidate.

Lula consistently emphasized that his economic mantra is stability, credibility, and predictability - qualities that Alckmin represents for the PT government.

In addition to Alckmin's support, Lula also gained the endorsement of five other parties - PCdoB, PSOL, Rede, Solidariedade, and PV - in the first round.

In this second stage, Lula garnered even more support, with the country's leading economists by his side, in addition to Senator Simone Tebet (MDB) - crucial for securing votes among Brazilian businessmen.

The 2022 presidential campaign in Brazil was

polarized between two candidates: Lula and Bolsonaro. Bolsonaro, wielding the power of the government and backed by several teams producing Fake News, continued to operate as he had over the past four years - spreading lies, denying responsibility for everything, and concocting falsehoods about Lula.

Shielded within evangelical temples and presenting his rhetoric as a means of religious worship, Bolsonaro maintained the support of millions of Brazilians, despite numerous complaints and committed crimes. These crimes included the genocide of the Yanomami indigenous population, the denial of over 80 emails from Pfizer (which wanted Brazil to be the first to receive vaccinations), resulting in months of delay and making Brazil the country with the highest proportion of Covid-19 deaths in the world - over 700,000 people. Bolsonaro's political career also saw the acquisition of more than 100 properties, with 51 of them purchased in cash. However, none of these revelations seemed to deter his fervent supporters, who were capable of committing various crimes, including murder and the invasion of buildings where the three federal powers operate, as evidenced by the events of January 8th.

The legacy of this fascist president to Brazil was one of terrorism.

Officially launched at the end of August 2022, the presidential campaigns provided valuable insights into the candidacies of Lula and Bolsonaro, even though they took place well before the second round was defined.

"At the PT campaign launch, we observed a somewhat nostalgic movement, with symbolic images that harkened back to 1989 - the year of Lula's first presidential campaign. Additionally, there was already an indication that they wanted to convey the idea of a broad front, with the inclusion of Alckmin - an important initial marker," evaluated political scientist Creomar de Souza, founder of the political consultancy Dharma.

In Bolsonaro's campaign, Souza believes that the highlight of the launch, which also set the tone for the current president's candidacy, was Michelle Bolsonaro's opening speeches. Over time, Michelle gradually became an important figure.

"To address one of his weak points, the rejection of female voters, the campaign chose his wife, Michelle, to take the stage. She played a prominent role in political advertising and on trips. She participated in dozens of evangelical services, singing the mantra of the struggle between 'good' (bolsonarism) and 'evil' (petismo). This strategy appears to have helped contain losses in this segment of the electorate," pointed out Professor Maria do Socorro Braga, who teaches Political Science at UFSCar (Federal University of São Carlos).

Bolsonaro concluded the first round of the presidential race with more votes than predicted by the polls. While research institutes indicated that the current president would secure around 37% of the votes, he advanced to the second round with 43.2%.

In an interview with BBC News Brasil, Sidney Chalhoub, a professor of History and African and Afro-American Studies at Harvard University in the United States, assessed that the vote showed the conservative reaction was not waning as previously thought.

According to the professor, the "conservative wave" could "survive democratically" and continue to influence democracy, despite its anti-democratic tendencies, due to its large number of supporters.

Politicians from Bolsonaro's party, PL, also won the majority of positions in Congress.

The party now holds the largest number of seats in the Chamber of Deputies, increasing from 76 current deputies to 99 in the next legislative term, as well as 14 seats in the Senate.

Lula secured important allies, extending beyond the expected names from the left. Among the support he received were former adversaries, such as the subtle support declared by Ciro Gomes (PDT) and the vocal and even militant support of Simone Tebet (MDB), who joined PT in rallies.

"The PT candidate managed to rally broad support from various social segments, including the low-income class, women from diverse professional fields, artists, celebrities, and parts of the economic, political, and financial elite," Professor Maria do Socorro Braga pointed out.

In the opinion of political scientist Creomar de Souza, Lula broke an ideological barrier by gaining support from figures considered to be from the center-right.

"Figures like Simone Tebet and Fernando Henrique Cardoso, who did not vote for the PT, represent something new in the political landscape. The support received by Bolsonaro so far is more of the same. There hasn't been anyone who stepped onto the podium that we could say, 'this was unexpected.'"

On October 14, during a podcast interview, Bolsonaro made controversial remarks when discussing a visit to a group of Venezuelan girls in the Federal District. He associated teenagers with sexual exploitation, stating, "There were about 15, 20 girls, Saturday morning, getting ready, all Venezuelan. I asked myself, pretty girls, 14, 15 years old, getting ready on a Saturday for what? To earn a living."

This speech stirred significant controversy. Supporters of the president quickly defended him, claiming that his words were taken out of context, and accused the left of spreading fake news.

The president also apologized if the phrases were "misunderstood" or caused "some kind of embarrassment to our Venezuelan sisters". Political scientist Camila Rocha, a researcher on the new right in Brazil at Cebrap, told the media that the apology was unprecedented.

"It's a strategy to humanize his figure because whoever does Bolsonaro's marketing realized that it has an important impact in terms of keeping people away from voting for Bolsonaro. He did it before, he's going to do it now - but it can give some result, yes. In the sense of someone who would even like to vote for Bolsonaro, then he saw the 'he painted a climate,' he was scared, but then he said 'okay, he apologized, or did something about it.'"

In the debate shown by a TV station on October 16, Bolsonaro and Lula spoke "face to face," without the intervention of third parties for a good part of the time, for the first time.

Lula focused part of his speech on his opponent's mismanagement of the COVID-19 pandemic and the economy, while Bolsonaro reinforced messages that linked his rival to corruption.

For Professor Maria do Socorro Braga, some debates harmed Lula.

"He didn't use his time well, especially in the last debate before the first round, and he even naively sought to place himself as a colleague of a politician who advocates decimating his opponent: Bolsonaro's accusations, pressures, and threats. Depending on the topics, he could have been more purposeful, strategic, and even unbalanced Bolsonaro," opines Braga.

"The 2022 election year was marked by the approval, by the Bolsonarist majority in Congress, of generous social benefits," recalls Professor Maria do Socorro Braga.

Informally known as the "package of goodness," these measures launched by the federal government to increase social expenses in the middle of the election period served to finance payroll loans, aid for families, and workers such as truck drivers and taxi drivers.

The measures were boosted in the last month, with the announcement of the anticipation of the last two installments of the aid paid to truck drivers and taxi drivers. It is estimated that the amount spent leaves a gap of BRL 68 billion in the Union's coffers in 2022 alone.

"These policies reached an extensive contingent of socially vulnerable people, undermining bases that in the past were courted by Lula."

On October 20, a resolution was approved stating that in cases of false news that have already been considered irregular by the members of the court, in a collegiate decision, the determination of removal from the air also applies to identical content replicated on the internet.

This means that if fake news with identical content to one already judged by the TSE begins to circulate, the president of the court, Alexandre de Moraes, can order it to go off the air without the need for a new action by parties, the Public Ministry, or a court decision with an application.

In another recent episode, "Jovem Pan," a radio and television company that had been including criticism of the former president in its daily programming, was prohibited from using terms such as "ex-convict" and "thief" in reference to Lula.

Jovem Pan published an editorial stating that "precisely those who should be one of the most solid pillars in the defense of democracy are today acting to weaken it, and they do this by relativizing the concepts of freedom of the press and expression, promoting the restriction of the free circulation of journalistic content, ideas, and opinions."

In an interview with BBC News Brasil, lawyer Alberto Rollo, specialized in electoral law, evaluates the expressions uttered by the broadcaster's commentators. "If one day I were convicted of something for which I could be called a thief and my lawsuit was annulled, it would be wrong to call me a thief empirically. resources]."

In the evaluation of Professor Luciana Veiga, Bolsonaro supporters saw the decision as a deprivation of liberty. "It was another point for the speech that their freedom of expression is at risk."

In the last week of the campaign, former deputy and Bolsonarist Roberto Jefferson, when he learned that he would be arrested by the Federal Police, fired more than 50 shots and threw three grenades at PF officials, who were injured.

"Jefferson is a declared supporter of Bolsonaro, and the predictable result was a negative side effect on the Bolsonarist campaign, hit by the effect of the shots. Especially since the victims were police officers, one of the bases that helped elect Bolsonaro in 2018. The violent attitude was followed by a first one, directed at a woman, the Minister of the Federal Supreme Court Cármen Lúcia, a public more resistant to Bolsonaro," says Braga.

Violence against Minister Carmem Lúcia, as mentioned by Braga, occurred during Jefferson's custody hearing on October 25th. In a statement to Airton Vieira, the judge investigating Justice Alexandre de Moraes at the Supreme Court, Jefferson referred to Cármen Lúcia in derogatory terms. He said that she acts "worse than prostitutes."

"This speech against a minister, specifically a woman in her sixties, had negative implications for Bolsonaro's gender strategy. Not to mention the issue of weapons," said Luciana Veiga.

Religion played a significant role in the recent dispute. False news stating that Lula intended to close churches was spread, prompting the PT (Workers' Party) to respond by meeting with priests and writing an open letter to evangelicals.

Meanwhile, Bolsonaro garnered support from evangelical influencers and maintained a strong backing within Christian communities.

The "tightening of social order in the religious field," as described by political scientist Luciana Veiga, proved to be a successful strategy for Bolsonaro.

"He primarily sought to align Christian, impoverished women from all over the country, especially the Northeast, based on their religious identities. This group, due to their social class and gender identity, could have been inclined to vote for Lula. However, Michelle and Bolsonaro made efforts to sway these women towards their side," Veiga explained.

One incident, however, tarnished the president's campaign. On October 12th, during celebrations honoring Our Lady of Aparecida, Bolsonaro supporters insulted and even booed a priest who advocated for combating hunger in the Basilica.

In the final stretch of the presidential elections' second round, Bolsonaro's re-election campaign appealed to the TSE (Superior Electoral Court), alleging that their ticket had been subject to "electoral fraud."

The alleged fraud was said to have occurred when radio stations in the North and Northeast regions ceased broadcasting thousands of campaign advertisements, which adversely affected the re-election candidate.

However, the Electoral Court dismissed the campaign's request for an investigation. In a statement released on Wednesday night, TSE President Alexandre de Moraes stated that the alleged irregularities were "inconsistent" and lacked "credible documentary evidence."

"Bolsonaro begins with the narrative that the

Electoral Court of Justice mishandled the radio advertisements and attempts to attribute this to Lula, suggesting, just days before the decision, that the elections were not clean," said Creomar de Souza.

According to Luciana Veiga, this allows Bolsonaro to provide his supporters with information that bolsters their strength on social media, where they had previously lost ground following the Roberto Jefferson incident. "Additionally, this creates another argument to question the election and promote discourse surrounding fraud if deemed necessary," she added.

Luiz Inácio Lula da Silva (PT) is now the President of the Republic for an unprecedented third term, having been elected with 59,563,912 votes (50.83% of valid votes). Jair Bolsonaro (PL) received 57,675,427 votes (49.17% of valid votes), making him the first president since the establishment of re-election in 2008 to not win a second term.

15

—

PRESIDENT ONCE AGAIN

ON OCTOBER 30, 2022, after two rounds of elections, fascist violence, and terrorism, Lula emerged victorious. This is the speech he gave after his victory was announced.

"My friends, we have reached the end of one of the most important elections in our history. An election that put two opposing projects for the country face to face, and that today has only one great winner: the Brazilian people.

This is not my victory, or the PT's victory, or the victory of the parties that supported me in this campaign. It is the victory of a huge democratic movement that was formed, above political parties, personal interests and ideologies, so that democracy could win.

On this historic October 30th, the majority of the Brazilian people made it clear that they want more democracy, not less.

They want more social inclusion and opportunities for all, not less. They want there to be more respect and understanding among Brazilians, not less. In short, they want more freedom, equality, and fraternity in our country, not less.

The Brazilian people showed today that they want more than to exercise their sacred right to choose who will govern their lives. They want to participate actively in the decisions of the government.

The Brazilian people showed today that they want more than just the right to protest that they are hungry, that there are no jobs, that their salary is insufficient to live with dignity, that they have no access to health and education, that they lack a roof over their heads to live and to raise their children safely, that there are no prospects for the future.

The Brazilian people want to live well, eat well, have a good home. They want a good job, a salary always adjusted above inflation, they want quality health care and public education.

They want religious freedom. They want books instead of guns. They want to go to the theater, see cinema, have access to all cultural activities, because culture feeds our soul.

The Brazilian people want hope back.

This is my understanding of democracy. Not just as a beautiful word written in law, but as something tangible, that we feel in our skin, and that we can build in everyday life.

It was this democracy, in the broadest sense of the term, that the Brazilian people chose today at the ballot box. It was this democracy – real, concrete – that we committed to throughout our campaign.

And it is this democracy that we will seek to build every day of our government. With economic growth distributed among the entire population, because this is how the economy should work – as an instrument to improve the lives of all, and not to perpetuate inequalities.

The wheel of the economy will begin to turn again, with job creation, wage appreciation and renegotiation of the debts of families who have lost their purchasing power.

The wheel of the economy will turn again with the poor included in the budget. With support for small and medium-sized rural producers, who are responsible for 70% of the food that reaches our tables.

With every possible incentive for micro and small entrepreneurs, so that they can put their extraordinary creative potential at the service of the country's development.

It is necessary to go further. Strengthen policies to combat violence against women, and ensure that women earn the same salaries as men for equal work.

To fight relentlessly against racism, prejudice and discrimination, so that whites, Blacks and Indigenous people have the same rights and opportunities.

This is the only way we will be able to build a country for all. An egalitarian Brazil, whose priority is the people who need it most.

A Brazil with peace, democracy and opportunities.

My friends, as of January 1, 2023, I will govern for 215 million Brazilians, and not only for those who voted for me. There are not two Brazils. We are a single country, a single people, a great nation.

It is of no interest to anyone to live in a family where discord reigns. It's time to bring families back together, to rebuild the bonds of friendship broken by the criminal spread of hate.

No one is interested in living in a divided country, in a permanent state of war.

This country needs peace and unity. The people do not want to fight anymore. The people are tired of seeing the other as an enemy to be feared or destroyed.

It's time to put down the weapons that should never have been taken up. Guns kill. And we choose life.

The challenge is immense. This country must be rebuilt in all its dimensions. In politics, in the economy, in public management, in institutional harmony, in international relations and, above all, in caring for the people most in need.

We must rebuild the very soul of this country. To recover generosity, solidarity, respect for differences, and love for one's neighbor.

To bring back the joy of being Brazilian, and the pride we always had in the Green and Yellow and the flag of our country. This Green and Yellow and this flag that belong to no one but the Brazilian people.

Our most urgent commitment is to end hunger again. We cannot accept as normal that millions of men, women and children in this country have nothing to eat, or that they consume fewer calories and proteins than necessary.

If we are the world's third largest producer of food and the first in animal protein, if we have technology and a huge amount of arable land, if we are able to export to the entire world, then we have the duty to guarantee that every Brazilian can have breakfast, lunch and dinner every day.

This will, once again, be the number one commitment of our government.

We cannot accept as normal that entire families are

forced to sleep on the streets, exposed to the cold, rain and violence.

Therefore, we will resume Minha Casa, Minha Vida (My House, My Life), with priority for low-income families, and bring back the social inclusion programs that lifted 36 million Brazilians out of extreme poverty.

Brazil can no longer live with this immense bottomless pit, this wall of concrete and inequality that separates Brazil into unequal parts that do not recognize each other. This country needs to recognize itself. It needs to reconnect with itself.

Beyond fighting extreme poverty and hunger, we are going to reestablish dialogue in this country.

We have to reestablish the dialogue with the Legislature and the Judiciary. Without attempts to exaggerate, intervene, control, or co-opt, but rather to rebuild a harmonious, republican coexistence among the three branches of government.

Democratic normality is consecrated in the Constitution. It establishes the rights and obligations of each power, each institution, the Armed Forces, and each one of us.

The Constitution governs our collective existence, and no one, absolutely no one, is above it, no one has the right to ignore it or to flout it.

It is also more urgent than ever to resume the dialogue between the people and the government.

That's why we shall bring back the national conferences. So that the interested parties can choose their priorities, and present the government with suggestions for public policies for each sector: education, health, security, women's rights, racial equality, youth, housing, and so many others.

Let's resume the dialogue with the governors and the mayors, to define together the priority public works for each population.

It doesn't matter which party the governor and the mayor belong to. Our commitment will always be to improve the lives of the people of each state and each municipality in this country.

We will also reestablish the dialogue between government, businessmen, workers and organized civil society, with the return of the Council for Economic and Social Development.

In other words, the major political decisions that impact the lives of 215 million Brazilians will not be made in secret, in the dead of night, but after a broad dialogue with society.

I believe that the main problems of Brazil, of the world, of the human being, can be solved with dialogue, and not with brute force.

Let no one doubt the power of the word, when it comes to seeking understanding and the common good.

My friends, in my international travels and in my meetings with leaders from many countries, what I hear most is that the world misses Brazil.

Longing for that sovereign Brazil, that spoke as an equal with the richest and most powerful countries. And that at the same time contributed to the development of the poorer countries.

The Brazil that supported the development of African countries, through cooperation, investment, and technology transfer.

Who worked for the integration of South America, Latin America and the Caribbean, who strengthened

Mercosur, and helped create the G20, UNASUR, CELAC and BRICS.

Today we say to the world that Brazil is back. That Brazil is too big to be relegated to this sad role of the world's pariah.

We will win back the credibility, the predictability and the stability of the country, so that investors – domestic and foreign – will regain confidence in Brazil. So that they stop seeing our country as a source of immediate and predatory profit, and become our partners in the resumption of economic growth with social inclusion and environmental sustainability.

We want fairer international trade. We want to resume our partnerships with the United States and the European Union on new terms. We are not interested in trade agreements that condemn our country to the eternal role of exporter of commodities and raw materials.

Let us re-industrialize Brazil, let us invest in the green and digital economy, let us support the creativity of our businessmen and entrepreneurs. We want to export knowledge as well.

We will fight again for new global governance, with the inclusion of more countries in the UN Security Council and with the end of the veto, which undermines the balance between nations.

We are ready to re-engage in the fight against hunger and inequality in the world, and in efforts to promote peace among peoples.

Brazil is ready to resume its protagonism in the fight against the climate crisis, protecting all of our ecosystems, especially the Amazon forest.

Under our government, we were able to reduce

deforestation in the Amazon by 80%, considerably reducing the emission of greenhouse gases.

Now, let's fight for zero deforestation of the Amazon.

Brazil and the planet need a living Amazon. A standing tree is worth more than tons of wood illegally extracted by those who think only of easy profit, at the expense of the deterioration of life on Earth.

A river of clean water is worth much more than all the gold extracted at the expense of mercury that kills animals and puts human life at risk.

When an Indigenous child is murdered by the greed of the exploiters of the environment, a part of humanity dies along with it.

For this reason, we will resume monitoring and surveillance of the Amazon, and combat any and all illegal activity – whether it be mining, logging or illegal agriculture.

At the same time, we will promote the sustainable development of the communities that live in the Amazon region. We will prove once again that it is possible to generate wealth without destroying the environment.

We are open to international cooperation to preserve the Amazon, whether in the form of investment or scientific research. But always under the leadership of Brazil, without ever renouncing our sovereignty.

We are committed to Indigenous peoples, to the other peoples of the forest, and to biodiversity. We want environmental peacemaking.

We are not interested in a war for the

environment, but we are ready to defend it from any threat.

My friends, the new Brazil that we will build on January 1st is not only of interest to the Brazilian people, but to all people who work for peace, solidarity and brotherhood, anywhere in the world.

Last Wednesday, Pope Francis sent an important message to Brazil, praying that the Brazilian people will be free of hatred, intolerance and violence.

I want to say that we wish the same, and we will work tirelessly for a Brazil where love prevails over hate, truth conquers lies, and hope is greater than fear.

Every day of my life I am reminded of the greatest teaching of Jesus Christ, which is to love your neighbor. So I believe that the most important virtue of a good leader will always be love – for his country and for his people.

As far as we are concerned, there is no lack of love in this country. We will take great care of Brazil and the Brazilian people. We will live in a new time. One of peace, of love and of hope.

A time when the Brazilian people will once again have the right to dream. And the opportunities to accomplish all that they dream of.

For this, I invite each and every Brazilian, regardless of which candidate they voted for in this election. More than ever, let's work together for Brazil, focusing on what unites us, rather than on our differences.

I know the scale of the mission that history has in store for me, and I know that I will not be able to fulfill it alone. I will need everyone – political parties, workers, businessmen, congressmen, governors, mayors, people of all religions. Brazilians who dream of a more developed, fairer, and more fraternal Brazil.

I will say again what I said during the whole campaign. Something that was never just the mere promise of a candidate, but a profession of faith, a lifetime commitment.

O Brasil tem jeito (Brazil has a way forward). All of us together will be able to fix this country, and build a Brazil the size of our dreams – with opportunities to transform them into reality.

Once again, I renew my eternal gratitude to the Brazilian people. A big hug, and may God bless our journey.'

16

A PROUD BRAZILIAN

WHAT KIND of challenges lie ahead for Lula and Brazil?

In 2002, when he defeated José Serra (PSDB) in the second round with 61% of the valid votes, Lula emphasized the power of alliances.

At that time, the PT's victory was only possible due to an alliance with conservative groups in Brazilian politics. Lula promised to implement pragmatic economic measures and assured that Brazil would honor all its commitments to foreign capital.

Lula assumed office on January 1, 2003, with an agenda that combined economic orthodoxy and increased social benefits. The Bolsa Família program played a crucial role in this regard.

Lula's first government was characterized by significant achievements for the Brazilian economy. These accomplishments include a reduction in public debt from 76% to 61% of GDP, a decrease in inflation from 12.5% in 2002 to 3.1% in 2006, and impressive GDP growth rates of 5.7% in 2004, 4% in 2006, and

6% in 2007. Additionally, Brazil's dollar reserves increased to approximately US$300 billion, the minimum wage rose from R$200 to R$540 over the course of eight years, and the unemployment rate dropped from 13% to 6%. The government also made strides in reducing social inequality, as evidenced by the decline in the Gini coefficient from 0.589 in 2002 to 0.527 in 2011. Moreover, an astounding 22 million people were lifted out of extreme poverty, while another 25 million joined the middle class.

These impressive economic outcomes solidified Lula's position for a second term. In 2006, he secured re-election by defeating Alckmin, who was affiliated with the PSDB party. Lula garnered 61% of the valid votes, while his opponent received 39% of the vote share.

Fast forward to 2022, Lula was elected once again, pledging to recreate the success of his 2002 government, albeit with some slight left-leaning adjustments. His primary goals encompass combating inflation, discontinuing Petrobras' international price parity policy, repealing the spending cap law, revoking regressive milestones within the existing labor legislation, reviewing pensions, implementing a tax reform that simplifies the system and adopts a progressive model, resuming public investments in infrastructure and housing, opposing privatization, and reallocating budgetary resources to benefit the most impoverished segments of society.

Lula's victory, however, faced opposition from supporters of Jair Bolsonaro, who refused to accept their candidate's defeat and advocated for a coup to maintain his grip on power. Such demands are illegal according to the Federal Constitution. These Bolsonaro supporters congregated in front of military barracks across various cities in Brazil.

This staunch radicalism among Bolsonaro's followers raised significant concerns about Lula's safety leading up to his inauguration. In the midst of this tense backdrop, Jair Bolsonaro made the decision to travel to the United States, abandoning his presidential duties in his final days in office. Consequently, Bolsonaro was absent from Lula's inauguration ceremony and did not partake in the traditional ceremony of passing the presidential sash, which symbolizes the transition of power. Bolsonaro's actions marked the first instance of a president during this era deviating from protocol.

On January 8, 2023, thousands of protesters congregated in Brasília, forcefully entering the "Praça dos Três Poderes" and wreaking havoc at the Planalto Palace, the National Congress, and the Federal Supreme Court. The destruction caused both structural and property damage, with estimates placing the cost in the millions of reais.

The attack on Brasilia was part of a coup attempt aimed at overthrowing Lula, allowing Bolsonaro to retain power. Investigations indicated the involvement of elements from the Armed Forces. Additionally, over a thousand individuals involved in the attack were apprehended. Several days later, a document was discovered, revealing that certain members of the Bolsonaro government had contemplated executing a coup to prevent Lula from assuming office.

At nearly 80 years old, Lula, who has been elected to the highest public office in one of the world's largest countries three times, has triumphed over cancer, political incarceration, a group of corrupt judges who orchestrated his arrest, media persecution, and a plot designed to end his career. Today, he stands as Brazil's president once again, possessing robust health and the wisdom that only someone who has emerged from poverty can bring.

The future remains uncertain, but Lula is undoubtedly one of the Brazilians who has relentlessly fought throughout his life to reach his current position, challenging the flawed and deceptive concept of meritocracy propagated by the Brazilian fascist conservative right.

He has endured the loss of his wife, a finger, and his freedom.

Yet, his dignity has never wavered.

Lula, a humble young trade unionist turned politician.

Above all, he is a proud Brazilian.